## COVER IMAGE SUMMARY

The cover of The Sacredness of Self-Love is a visual embodiment of divine self-love and spiritual awakening. A radiant feminine figure sits in serene stillness, enveloped in a warm glow, symbolizing inner peace and sacred energy. A soft, ethereal light emanates from her heart and womb space, representing the powerful connection between self-love and divine creation. The celestial backdrop reflects the vastness of the cosmos, reminding us that within each of us exists the infinite universe of love, wisdom, and healing.

This imagery reflects the essence of the book—a journey of self-discovery, celibacy as a sacred commitment, and the awakening of divine feminine and masculine balance. It invites the reader to embrace their own sacredness and step into a life of wholeness, empowerment, and unconditional love.

Copyright © 2025 by Empress Nefertiti-Mumbi
All rights reserved. No part of this book may be reproduced, distributed, or transmitted in any form or by any means, including photocopying, recording, or other electronic or mechanical methods, without the prior written permission of the author, except in the case of brief quotations embodied in critical reviews and certain other noncommercial uses permitted by copyright law.

ISBN: 979-8-9924327-0-1
Publisher: Sacred Essence Press
First Edition: 2025
Printed in the United States of America

This book is published with the intent to inspire, guide, and empower readers.
It is not intended as a substitute for professional advice or therapy.
The author and publisher disclaim any liability for the use or misuse of the material in this book.

This book is dedicated to the beautiful souls who seek love, not in the world around them, but within the sacred sanctuary of their own hearts. May these pages awaken the infinite wellspring of love that has always been yours, guiding you to embrace your essence and radiate it into the universe. May you find healing, wholeness, and the purest expression of self-love.

# Acknowledgment

To Wisdom,

My unwavering guide and source of infinite inspiration.

Thank you for your steadfast support, unconditional care and the boundless wisdom you share so freely.

Your light has graced my journey, illuminating my path of healing and creation. This book is a reflection of your encouragement, a celebration of our shared truths, and a testament to the beauty of your enduring love.

With all my gratitude,

Empress Nefertiti-Mumbi

*"Each chapter is infused with divine energy. Every word, reflection, and affirmation carries the essence of cosmic love and higher wisdom. It's a gift to the world."*

**ABOUT**

# Empress Nefertiti-Mumbi

Empress is a devoted wisdom keeper, healer, and storyteller, dedicated to guiding souls toward self-love, healing, and spiritual awakening. Rooted in ancient traditions and sacred knowledge, her work embodies the essence of divine wisdom, honoring the power of celibacy, natural healing, and the reconnection to one's true self.

Through her writings, music, and teachings, Empress inspires others to embrace their innate power, walk in sovereignty, and cultivate a life of deep inner peace and divine alignment. Her mission is to share the timeless truths of healing and self-discovery, illuminating the path for those seeking wholeness, love, and transformation.

# THE SACREDNESS OF SELF-LOVE

## CONTENTS

1. **Honoring Your Inner Self as Sacred**

2. **Developing a Deeper Relationship with Yourself**

3. **Creating Rituals for Self-Connection**

4. **Celibacy as Sacred Self-Love: Transmuting Energy into Divine Creativity**

# Table of Contents

## 01 — Page 8
### HONORING YOUR INNER SELF AS SACRED
You are your own sacred space—a sanctuary for peace, growth, and healing.

## 02 — Page 65
### DEVELOPING A DEEPER RELATIONSHIP WITH YOURSELF
You can develop a deeper sense of self-love by treating yourself with the same patience and kindness that you would show someone you care about.

## 03 — Page 102
### CREATING RITUALS FOR SELF-CONNECTION
Simple, everyday actions carried out with intention create a sacred rhythm that stimulates inner love and trust.

## 04 — Page 121
### CELIBACY AS SACRED SELF-LOVE:
### TRANSMUTING ENERGY INTO DIVINE CREATIVITY
Celibacy as an act of self-love and a spiritual practice.

## 05 — Page 181
### CONCLUSION
Congratulations on completing this journey of Honoring Your Inner Self as Sacred.

# CHAPTER 01

> Celibacy as a path to self-love creates the possibility to nourish, honor, and deeply connect to oneself. This journey is about seeing self-love as more than just kindness or compassion for oneself, but as a sacred act of reverence that creates an inner sanctuary.

@ Empress Nefertiti-Mumbi

# HONORING YOUR INNER SELF AS SACRED

*You are your own sacred space—a sanctuary for peace, growth, and healing.*

**Overview:**
This section invites you to see your inner self as a temple. Encouraging you to protect, nurture, and cherish your personal space can increase appreciation and respect throughout your unique journey.

**Extended Insight:**
When we honor ourselves as sacred, every choice we make, from what we eat to how we speak to ourselves, becomes an act of love. This shift in perspective transforms daily decisions into acts of love.

**Additional Practical Tips:**
*Sacred Boundary Setting:* Encourage you to honor your personal boundaries as sacred. This could entail taking the time to reflect on what you need to be balanced and gently but firmly communicating those needs to others

*Self-Acknowledgment Exercise:* At the end of each day, take a few minutes to reflect on one or two things you carried out well or admire about yourself. This activity increases inner confidence as well as self-worth.

*Affirmation:* "I honor my worth by choosing what nourishes my mind, body, and spirit. Each decision I make is a step toward my highest self. I say yes to myself with love, confidence, and joy."

*Extended Journaling Prompts*
- "In what ways can I treat myself with the same care and devotion that I would offer a loved one?"
- "What boundaries can I set to honor my sacred inner space, and how can I maintain them with love and compassion?

# HONORING YOUR INNER SELF AS SACRED

*Honoring your inner self as sacred is essential for self-love and harmonious connections with others.*

**You Are the Foundation of Your Life:**

Everything you create, achieve, or contribute comes from your relationship with yourself. If this foundation is weakened—if you ignore your wants, your emotions, or your worth—your ability to sustain anything significant is compromised. Honoring oneself enhances the foundation, creating harmony and balance.

**Healing Is Essential for True Service:**

It is impossible to pour from an empty cup. When you are not healed, your energy becomes fractured, and helping others might feel exhausting or transactional. By focusing on your healing, you allow yourself to serve from a place of wholeness, ensuring that all of your actions uplift others without exhausting yourself.

**Self-Love Is the Blueprint for All Relationships:**

How you treat yourself sets the basis for how others treat you. Loving yourself teaches you how to set boundaries, communicate your needs, and identify healthy love in others. Without this inner blueprint, relationships may may lack authenticity and mutual respect.

**Love Starts Within and Radiates Outward:**

True love is abundant and vast, yet it starts within. When you truly love yourself, you exude calm confidence and a kind energy that naturally raises others. Self-love enhances rather than diminishes your ability to contribute.

**Choosing Yourself First**

Choosing yourself is sacred, not selfish. It is an act of reclaiming your power, affirming your worth, and committing to your own well-being. This does not imply ignoring others; rather, it is a vow to be your best self, which will benefit everyone in your life.

**Example Analogy:**

Imagine you are a gardener. How can you offer flowers or fruits if you neglect your own garden, allowing the soil to dry and weeds to grow? Caring for yourself first guarantees that you have beauty and sustenance to offer the world

# HONORING YOUR INNER SELF AS SACRED

*Honoring your inner self as sacred is essential for self-love and harmonious connections with others.*

**Practical Actions for Choosing Yourself**

Everything you create, achieve, or contribute comes from your relationship with yourself. If this foundation is weakened—if you ignore your wants, your emotions, or your worth—your ability to sustain anything significant is compromised. Honoring oneself enhances the foundation, creating harmony and balance.

- **Say Yes to Yourself:** When faced with choices, ask yourself, "Does this promote my well-being? Is this consistent with my values? Prioritize decisions that will help you grow and find serenity.

- **Schedule Sacred Time:** Set aside time each day or weekly for things that nourish you, such as journaling, meditating, going for a walk, or simply resting. Consider this time non-negotiable.

- **Release What No Longer Serves:** Let go of people, habits and commitments that are draining you. This act of releasing is an aspect of self-respect that creates space for what is truly meaningful.

**Benefits of Honoring Your Inner Self**

- **Clarity of Purpose:** When you connect with yourself, your goals and values become clear. This clarity allows you to make decisions that are in alignment with your highest good.
- **Deeper Connections:** Loving yourself teaches you how to have healthier, more fulfilling relationships that are free of reliance and insecurity.
- **Inner Peace:** Honoring oneself provides a tremendous sense of calm since you no longer seek validation or fulfillment from other sources.
- **Resilience:** With a strong sense of self, you are more equipped to face obstacles with poise and confidence.

# Say Yes to Yourself

VISUALIZATION EXERCISE:
YES TO YOURSELF

## Find a Quiet Space:

Sit comfortably, close your eyes, and take three deep, grounding breaths. Inhale deeply through your nose, filling your chest and belly, and exhale slowly through your mouth.

## Affirmation with Visualization:

Imagine you're holding a beautiful balloon in your hands. This balloon represents all that no longer serves you—whether it's a habit, relationship, fear, or limiting belief.

As you breathe deeply, imagine a golden light radiating from your heart. This light represents your love and commitment to yourself.

Silently or aloud, repeat the affirmation:

"I honor my worth by choosing what nourishes my mind, body, and spirit. Each decision I make is a step toward my highest self. I say yes to myself with love, confidence, and joy."

With each word, visualize the golden light growing brighter, spreading warmth throughout your body, and enveloping you in a protective and loving glow.

## Anchor the Feeling:

Place your hands over your heart and feel the warmth of your light. Say, "I am worthy of love, care, and peace. Choosing myself is my sacred right."

Open your eyes, carry this radiant energy forward, and let it guide your decisions throughout the day.

**This exercise can be done daily or whenever you need a reminder of your inner power and worthiness.**

# Release What No Longer Serves:

## VISUALIZATION EXERCISE: LETTING GO WITH LOVE

### Prepare Your Space:

Sit or stand in a quiet place where you won't be disturbed. Close your eyes and take three deep breaths, inhaling peace and exhaling tension.

### Connect with the Energy of Release:

Imagine you're holding a beautiful balloon in your hands. This balloon represents all that no longer serves you—whether it's a habit, relationship, fear, or limiting belief.

### Affirmation with Release:

Silently or aloud, say;

"I lovingly release all that no longer serves my highest good.
I let go with gratitude, creating space for joy, peace, and love to flow into my life."

As you say this, visualize gently letting the balloon go. Watch it rise into the sky, becoming smaller and smaller, until it disappears completely.

### Anchor the Feeling:

Place your hands on your heart and take a deep breath. Feel the lightness of letting go. Say,

"I am free. I am open. I am ready to embrace all that aligns with my highest self."

### Conclude with Gratitude:

Smile gently, knowing you've created space for new blessings and opportunities.

CHAPTER 01

# JOURNAL

## HONORING YOUR INNER SELF AS SACRED

THE SACREDNESS OF SELF-LOVE

# Self-Reflection

1. What does it mean to me to honor myself as sacred?

# Self-Reflection

# Self-Reflection

## 2. When do I feel most connected to my true essence?

# Self-Reflection

## Self-Reflection

*3. What are the parts of myself I tend to neglect, and how can I nurture them?*

# Self-Reflection

# Self-Reflection

*4. What are three things I deeply love about myself?*

# Self-Reflection

# Self-Reflection

*5. How do I define self-love, and how can I embody it more fully?*

# Self-Reflection

# Embracing Your Worth

6. What limiting beliefs am I ready to release about my worth?

# Embracing Your Worth

# Embracing Your Worth

**7. How can I set boundaries that honor my emotional and physical well-being?**

_____
_____
_____
_____
_____
_____
_____
_____
_____
_____
_____
_____
_____
_____
_____
_____
_____
_____

# Embracing Your Worth

# Embracing Your Worth

*8. What does saying 'yes' to myself look like in my daily life?*

# Embracing Your Worth

# Embracing Your Worth

9. What are five ways I can prioritize my needs without guilt?

# Embracing Your Worth

# Embracing Your Worth

**10. How do I celebrate my uniqueness and divine essence?**

# Embracing Your Worth

# Connecting with Your Sacred Space

*11. What rituals or practices make me feel connected to my inner self?*

# Connecting with Your Sacred Space

# Connecting with Your Sacred Space

*12. What kind of environment helps me feel at peace and sacred within myself?*

# Connecting with Your Sacred Space

# Connecting with Your Sacred Space

*13. How can I create a sacred morning or evening routine?*

# Connecting with Your Sacred Space

# Connecting with Your Sacred Space

## 14. What is one small action I can take daily to honor my inner sanctuary?

# Connecting with Your Sacred Space

# Connecting with Your Sacred Space

15. What colors, scents, or symbols resonate with my sacred essence?

# Connecting with Your Sacred Space

# Healing and Growth

**16. What emotions or past experiences am I ready to heal and let go of?**

# Healing and Growth

# Healing and Growth

17. How have I grown through challenging times, and how can I honor that growth?

# Healing and Growth

## Healing and Growth

18. What is a lesson I've learned about self-love that has changed me?

# Healing and Growth

# Healing and Growth

19. Who or what inspires me to treat myself with more kindness and care?

# Healing and Growth

# Healing and Growth

*20. How can I show gratitude to my body, mind, and spirit today?*

# Healing and Growth

# Expanding into Sacred Living

*21. What habits or practices bring me closer to living in alignment with my highest self?*

# Expanding into Sacred Living

# Expanding into Sacred Living

## 22. What does honoring my spiritual essence look like in my daily interactions?

# Expanding into Sacred Living

# Expanding into Sacred Living

*23. How can I embody love and light in my relationships while staying true to myself?*

# Expanding into Sacred Living

# Expanding into Sacred Living

*24. What activities help me feel more alive, vibrant, and connected to the divine?*

# Expanding into Sacred Living

# Expanding into Sacred Living

*25. If I could write a letter to my future self, what words of love and encouragement would I include?*

# Expanding into Sacred Living

# CHAPTER 02

> Forgiveness, and open communication are all components of a loving relationship with oneself, as they are in any other intimate connection.
>
> @ Empress Nefertiti-Mumbi

# DEVELOPING A DEEPER RELATIONSHIP WITH YOURSELF

*Treat yourself with the same patience and kindness that you would show someone you care about.*

**Overview:**
The second section reinforces self-support, guidance, and comfort for oneself. It emphasizes that self-love is not just an emotion, but a continuous relationship that needs regular attention and kindness.

**Extended Insight:**
Understanding, forgiveness, and open communication are all components of a loving relationship with oneself, as they are in any other intimate connection. Learning to "show up" for oneself every day boosts self-esteem and cultivates resilience.

**Additional Practical Tips:**

**Mirror Work:** Spend a few minutes every day looking in the mirror and expressing thanks or positive affirmations to yourself. This practice can be empowering and grounding.

**Emotional Check-In Journal:** Keep a journal just for emotional reflections. Each evening, write a few words on how you felt that day, which emotions were most intense, and what those emotions could be asking of you.

**Affirmation:** "I am in harmony with myself and my truth."

**Extended Journaling Prompts**
- "What does it mean to 'show up' for myself, and how can I honor this commitment daily?"
- "What are three qualities I love and appreciate about myself, and how can I celebrate them?"

# DEVELOPING A DEEPER RELATIONSHIP WITH YOURSELF

*Treat yourself with the same patience and kindness that you would show someone you care about.*

Creating a deep connection with yourself is an essential element of self-love and joy. It allows you to live authentically, trust your intuition, and honor your unique essence.

**Understanding the Importance of Self-Connection:**

***Why It Matters:*** Having a deeper connection with yourself promotes inner serenity and clarity. It builds a solid basis for meaningful relationships with others. When you truly know and love yourself, you become more resilient, confident, and aligned with your purpose.

***Reflection Question:*** What does it mean to truly know myself?

**Practices to Foster Self-Connection:**

**a. *Daily Quietude:***
- Spend 10-15 minutes daily in stillness or meditation.
- Focus on your breath, gently observing your thoughts without judgment.
- Use affirmations like, *"I am in harmony with myself and my truth."*

**b. *Mirror Work:***
- Stand before a mirror, look into your eyes, and speak words of kindness and affirmation.
- **Example:** *"I see you, I value you, I honor your journey."*

**c. *Journaling for Self-Discovery:***
- Explore your emotions, experiences, and thoughts through daily journaling.
- **Ask:** *What brings me joy? What triggers discomfort? What does my heart long for?*

**d. *Ritual of Gratitude:***
- Each morning or evening, list three things you appreciate about yourself or your life.
- Gratitude raises your vibration and deepens your relationship with your inner self.

**Reconnecting with Your Inner Child:**
- Visualize your younger self. What did they dream about? What brought them joy?
- Write a letter of love and encouragement to your inner child.
- Embrace playful activities you once loved, such as drawing, dancing, or exploring nature.

# DEVELOPING A DEEPER RELATIONSHIP WITH YOURSELF

*Treat yourself with the same patience and kindness that you would show someone you care about.*

**Reconnecting with Your Inner Child:**
- Visualize your younger self. What did they dream about? What brought them joy?
- Write a letter of love and encouragement to your inner child.
- Embrace playful activities you once loved, such as drawing, dancing, or exploring nature.

**Unveiling and Releasing False Identities:**

*Recognizing Conditioning:* Reflect on beliefs or habits that may have been imposed by society, family, or peers.

*Releasing:* Practice forgiveness and letting go through affirmations like, "I release what is not mine to carry."

*Replace outdated narratives with empowering truths.*

**Building Trust Within:**

*Follow Through:* Keep small promises to yourself to build trust in your own word.

*Self-Validation:* Instead of seeking approval externally, affirm your own choices and actions.

*Reflection:* How can I honor myself today?

**Embodying Sacred Self-Care:**

Treat your body and soul as sacred. Nourish yourself with:
- **Physical Care:** Eat wholesome foods, move your body, and rest well.
- **Emotional Care:** Allow space for your feelings without judgment.
- **Energetic Care:** Cleanse your space and aura with incense, sage, or sound bowls.

**Engaging in Heartfelt Self-Dialogue:**

*Practice Loving Questions:* Ask yourself daily, What do I need? What am I feeling? How can I nurture myself today?

Listen to the answers with compassion and respond with action.

# DEVELOPING A DEEPER RELATIONSHIP WITH YOURSELF

*Treat yourself with the same patience and kindness that you would show someone you care about.*

**Celebrating Yourself Regularly:**
- Acknowledge your growth and accomplishments, no matter how small.
- Create a "celebration jar" where you write down your wins and revisit them during challenging times.

**Embracing Solitude:**
- View time alone as an opportunity for intimacy with yourself.
- Use solitude to explore hobbies, meditate, or simply rest in your own presence.
- Affirmation: *"In my own company, I find peace and wisdom."*

**Aligning with Your Soul's Desires:**
- Revisit your passions and dreams. What lights up your spirit?
- Take inspired action to pursue activities that align with your soul's calling.
- Reminder: *"When I honor my desires, I honor my soul."*

**How to Deepen Your Mirror Work Practice:**
- ***Morning Ritual:*** Start each day with 1-3 affirmations to set a loving tone for the day.
- ***Evening Reflection:*** End the day by thanking yourself for your efforts and growth.
- ***Emotional Presence:*** Allow tears or emotions to flow freely during the process. This is a sign of a deeper connection.
- ***Touch Connection:*** Place your hands over your heart or gently touch your face as you affirm your love.

**Suggestions for Creating a Sacred Space:**

### 1. Location
- Choose a quiet, private area where you feel safe and undisturbed.
- Ideally, the space should have a mirror you can sit or stand in front of comfortably.
- If possible, choose a spot near natural light for a soothing, uplifting ambiance.

### 2. Clearing the Energy

- ***Incense or Smudging:*** Use sage, palo santo, or your favorite incense (e.g., lavender for calm or sandalwood for grounding) to cleanse the area energetically.

# DEVELOPING A DEEPER RELATIONSHIP WITH YOURSELF

*Treat yourself with the same patience and kindness that you would show someone you care about.*

- **Sound Clearing:** Ring a bell, chime, or use a singing bowl to release stagnant energy.
- **Intentional Cleaning:** Physically clean the area while visualizing negativity being swept away.

### 3. Setting the Mood

- **Lighting:** Use soft lighting like candles, fairy lights, or a salt lamp for a warm glow.
- **Textures:** Add a soft rug, cushions, or a comfortable chair to make the space inviting.
- **Decor:** Incorporate elements that inspire you, such as fresh flowers, crystals, or meaningful artwork.

### 4. Sacred Items

- **Mirror:** Keep the mirror clean and dedicated to your self-love rituals. You may want to frame it with lights or decorative accents.
- **Crystals:**
  - **Rose Quartz:** For self-love and compassion.
  - **Amethyst:** For spiritual connection and calming energy.
  - **Citrine:** For confidence and inner joy.
- **Affirmation Cards:** Place your favorite affirmations nearby for inspiration.
- **Symbols of Divinity:** Include items that represent your spirituality, such as statues, sacred geometry, or cultural symbols.

### 5. Aromatherapy

- Use essential oils in a diffuser or anoint your pulse points.
  - **Lavender:** For relaxation and calm.
  - **Frankincense:** For grounding and spiritual connection.
  - **Citrus Oils:** For uplifting and energizing.

### 6. Adding Sound

- **Music:** Play soft instrumental, binaural beats, or affirmational chants in the background.
- **Silence:** If you prefer silence, use noise-canceling headphones to block external noise.

# DEVELOPING A DEEPER RELATIONSHIP WITH YOURSELF

*Treat yourself with the same patience and kindness that you would show someone you care about.*

## 7. Ritual Enhancements

- ***Journaling:*** Keep a journal in the space to record insights or emotions after your practice.
- ***Water Element:*** Include a small bowl of water or a fountain to symbolize cleansing and flow.
- ***Sacred Cloth or Altar:*** Drape a beautiful cloth and arrange your items like a sacred altar.

## 8. Daily Intention Setting

- Before starting, set a clear intention for your practice, such as healing, self-acceptance, or love.
- Speak your intention aloud or silently as you light a candle or hold a crystal.

**Example Ritual: Mirror Work in Your Sacred Space:**
- Light a candle and cleanse the space with incense.
- Sit in front of the mirror, holding a rose quartz crystal.
- Speak your affirmations, looking deeply into your eyes.
- Place your hands over your heart and breathe deeply, feeling the energy flow through you.
- Conclude with gratitude, blowing out the candle to seal the practice.

**How to Integrate Sacred Symbols into Your Space**

Integrating sacred symbols into your sacred space helps to ground your practice in greater significance, spirituality, and personal connection. Here's how to strategically incorporate symbols that resonate with your ideas, culture, and intentions:

**1. Choose Symbols That Resonate**

- ***Cultural or Spiritual Symbols:*** Select symbols from your heritage or spiritual tradition, such as the Ankh (life and divine energy), Om (universal vibration), or a cross.
- ***Nature Symbols:*** Incorporate natural elements like feathers (freedom and *connection*), stones, or plants (growth and grounding).
- ***Universal Symbols:*** Use sacred geometry (e.g., the Flower of Life, Mandalas) or celestial icons like the moon and stars.

# DEVELOPING A DEEPER RELATIONSHIP WITH YOURSELF

*Treat yourself with the same patience and kindness that you would show someone you care about.*

### 2. Placement with Intention

- Place symbols in areas where your eyes naturally fall during your practice.
- Arrange them around your mirror, on your altar, or at eye level to amplify their energy.
- Use symmetry or circular arrangements to evoke balance and harmony.

### 3. Infuse with Energy

- **Consecration Ritual:** Cleanse your symbols with smoke, salt, or water to clear previous energies. Set intentions for their use in your sacred space.
- **Meditation:** Hold each symbol in your hands and meditate on its meaning, visualizing it radiating positive energy.
- **Affirmations:** Speak affirmations over them, such as, "This symbol anchors my intention for love and strength."

### 4. Incorporate in Specific Ways

1. **Altars or Tables:** Dedicate a small area to symbols, such as statues, meaningful objects, or tokens from loved ones.
2. **Wall Art:** Hang or paint sacred symbols, like mandalas or cultural icons, as a backdrop.
3. **Candles:** Use candles imprinted with symbols, or carve them directly onto the wax before lighting.
4. **Jewelry or Wearables:** Place symbolic necklaces, rings, or bracelets in your space to wear during rituals.
5. **Mirror Accents:** Frame your mirror with decals, charms, or engravings of symbols for an enhanced reflective experience.

### 5. Align Symbols with Your Intentions

- *For Self-Love:*
  - **Rose:** Represents love and beauty. Place fresh roses or rose-shaped objects in the space.
  - **Heart Shape:** Incorporate heart-shaped crystals, carvings, or art pieces.
- *For Spiritual Connection:*
  - **Lotus:** Symbolizes enlightenment and spiritual awakening. Include a lotus statue or design.
  - **Moon Phases:** Represent emotional cycles and transformation. Use moon phase illustrations or décor.

# DEVELOPING A DEEPER RELATIONSHIP WITH YOURSELF

*Treat yourself with the same patience and kindness that you would show someone you care about.*

- **For Strength and Protection:**

  - **Ankh:** Place an ankh near your mirror or wear one during your practice.
  - **Eye of Horus:** Include images or pendants to represent protection and clarity.

## 6. Personalize the Symbols

- **Family Heirlooms:** Use objects passed down from loved ones that carry significant energy or meaning.
- **Handmade Items:** Create or draw your own sacred symbols to infuse them with personal energy.
- **Sacred Texts:** Display or open a meaningful book, poem, or passage related to your practice.

## 7. Integrate Symbols into Rituals

- **Lighting Candles:** Use candles carved with symbols or anoint them with oils to amplify their power.
- **Daily Affirmations:** Incorporate symbols into spoken affirmations, e.g., holding an Ankh while saying,

  "I honor the divine energy of life within me."

- **Visualization:** Gaze at a symbol while meditating, visualizing its energy infusing your being.

## Example Sacred Symbols & Their Meanings

| Symbol | Meaning | Suggested Use |
|---|---|---|
| Ankh | Eternal life, Divine Feminine | Near the mirror or worn as jewelry |
| Lotus Flower | Spiritual growth, Purity | As art or a small statue on your altar |
| Feather | Ma'at, Freedom, spiritual messages | Placed in a vase or on your table |
| Tree of Life | Interconnectedness, strength | Wall art or carved onto wood |
| Moon | Cycles, intuition, feminine energy | Decorative phases or crystal carvings |
| Rose | Love, self-compassion | Fresh blooms or rose quartz crystals |

# MIRROR WORK AFFIRMATIONS:

Mirror work affirmations can help you strengthen your self-love and cultivate a sacred relationship with yourself. These affirmations are intended to resonate strongly when spoken while looking into one's own eyes.

### Self-Acceptance & Love
- "I see you, I honor you, and I love you exactly as you are."
- "You are worthy of love, joy, and every beautiful thing life has to offer."
- "I accept myself fully and unconditionally in this moment."

### Healing & Forgiveness
- "I forgive myself for past mistakes and embrace the lessons they've taught me."
- "Every part of me deserves compassion and kindness."
- "I release guilt and replace it with self-love."

### Empowerment & Strength
- "You are powerful, resilient, and capable of achieving your dreams."
- "I trust myself to make the best decisions for my life."
- "I am the creator of my reality and the artist of my life."

### Inner Beauty & Radiance
- "You are a reflection of divine beauty, inside and out."
- "My light shines brighter each day, and the world is better because of it."
- "I radiate love, confidence, and grace."

### Authenticity & Inner Truth
- "I honor my truth and live authentically in every moment."
- "I embrace all that I am and celebrate my unique essence."
- "I trust my intuition and follow the guidance of my soul."

### Gratitude & Abundance
- "Thank you for carrying me through every challenge and triumph."
- "I am grateful for this body, this mind, and this spirit."
- "Abundance flows effortlessly into my life because I am worthy."

### Sacred Connection with Self
- "I am my greatest ally, my deepest love, and my most sacred connection."
- "In my reflection, I see the sacred essence of who I am."
- "I am whole, I am sacred, and I am enough."

CHAPTER 02

# JOURNAL
## DEVELOPING A DEEPER RELATIONSHIP WITH YOURSELF

THE SACREDNESS OF SELF-LOVE

Today's date _____

# What does it mean to truly know myself?

Today's date _____

**What are some negative thought patterns that I tend to fall into, and how can I challenge or reframe them?**

Today's date _____

## What brings me joy?

Today's date _____

## What triggers discomfort?

Today's date _____

# What does my heart long for?

Today's date _____

## What do I need?

Today's date _____

# What am I feeling?

Today's date _____

## How can I nurture myself today?

Today's date _____

Today's date _____

Today's date _____

Today's date _____

Today's date

Today's date _____

Today's date _____

Today's date _____

Today's date _____

Today's date _____

Today's date _____

Today's date _____

Today's date _____

Today's date _____

Today's date _____

Today's date _____

Today's date _____

The Sacredness of Self-Love

# SELF CARE IS A PRIORITY AND Necessity NOT A LUXURY

Developing a Deeper Relationship with Yourself

# CHAPTER 03

> Rituals are powerful tools for creating consistency and intention, fostering a sense of stability and calm.

**@ Empress Nefertiti-Mumbi**

# CREATING RITUALS FOR SELF-CONNECTION

*These rituals, crafted with love and intention, create a foundation for nurturing a deeper connection to yourself.*

**Overview:**
Self-connection rituals create a routine that enables readers to devote more time to themselves, even in modest ways. This section teaches that rituals are powerful tools for creating consistency and intention, fostering a sense of stability and calm.

**Extended Insight:**
Rituals provide meaning to everyday activities, transforming them into symbols of love and peace. These tiny deeds remind us of our worth and help us be present in the moment.

**Additional Practical Tips:**

*Mindful Morning Practice:* Encourage you to spend the first few minutes of your day doing something relaxing, such as drinking a nice cup of tea, stretching, or simply watching sunrise. This is an opportunity to begin the day in peace and presence.

*Intention Candle Ritual:* Light a candle every evening with the goal of self-love, such as "I am enough" or "I am deserving of peace." Allowing the candle to burn for a few minutes while you reflect on your purpose can become a relaxing and pleasant habit.

*Affirmation:* "I am worthy of love."

**Extended Journaling Prompts**
- "What small, meaningful acts can I incorporate into my daily routine to remind myself of my value?"
- "How did my rituals today help me feel more connected to myself, and how can I expand them?

# CREATING RITUALS FOR SELF-CONNECTION

*These rituals, crafted with love and intention, create a foundation for nurturing a deeper connection to yourself.*

Creating rituals for self-connection is a lovely way to nourish your soul, honor your inner self, and cultivate a stronger feeling of love and awareness. Below is an expanded guide with thoughtful processes and suggestions for establishing meaningful rituals.

### 1. Understand the Purpose of Your Ritual

Think about why you're making this ritual. Are you looking for clarity, healing, self-love, grounding, or just connecting with your inner essence?

*Example intentions:*
- "To nurture self-love and acceptance."
- "To reconnect with my inner wisdom."
- "To create a sacred pause in my busy day."

### 2. Choose a Sacred Space

Dedicate a physical or symbolic space for your ritual. This might be:
- A section of your space decorated with meaningful items.
- An area in nature that makes you feel grounded.
- A mental space you imagine when meditating.

### Enhance Your Space

Use items that evoke a sense of sacredness:
- **Candles:** Representing illumination and focus.
- **Crystals:** Choose one based on your intention (e.g., rose quartz for self-love, amethyst for clarity).
- **Sacred Symbols:** Include symbols like an ankh, lotus, or infinity sign.
- **Incense or Essential Oils:** Burn incense or diffuse oils to create a soothing atmosphere. Lavender, sandalwood, or frankincense are wonderful options.

### 3. Create a Beginning Ritual (Grounding)

Begin with a technique that redirects your attention from external distractions to inward focus.
- **Centering Breath:** Take deep breaths, inhaling for 4 counts, holding for 4 counts, and exhaling for 6 counts.
- **Sound Clearing:** Ring a bell, chime, or play a singing bowl to clear the energy.
- **Affirmation Invocation:** Speak an affirmation to set the tone, such as:

"I honor this moment as sacred and welcome connection with my truest self."

# CREATING RITUALS FOR SELF-CONNECTION

*These rituals, crafted with love and intention, create a foundation for nurturing a deeper connection to yourself.*

**4. Incorporate a Practice to Connect**

Create the center of your ritual based on what is most meaningful to you.

*Examples:*

*a. Mirror Work:*
- Sit or stand in front of a mirror.
- Look into your own eyes and speak affirmations aloud, such as:
- "I see you. I honor you. I love you."
- "You are enough just as you are."
- Pause to observe any emotions or thoughts that arise.

*b. Journaling Ritual:*
- Write in a sacred journal using a specific prompt:
- "What do I need to feel whole today?"
- "What is something I deeply appreciate about myself?"
- Use a colored pen or special notebook that feels intentional.

*c. Self-Compassion Meditation:*

Visualize holding yourself in love. Imagine a warm, golden light surrounding your body, symbolizing acceptance and care.

*d. Movement as Ritual:*

Practice yoga, dance, or gentle stretching with the goal of honoring your body and spirit.

*e. Artistic Expression:*

Paint, sketch, or make anything that expresses your emotions or what you wish to let go of.

**5. Closing the Ritual**

Finish with a symbolic act that seals your connection.

*Examples:*
- Blow out a candle with gratitude for the time spent.
- Thank yourself aloud: "Thank you for showing up for me today."
- Place your hands over your heart, feel your heartbeat, and say: "I carry this connection with me always."
- Drink water or tea to symbolize integration and renewal.

# CREATING RITUALS FOR SELF-CONNECTION

*These rituals, crafted with love and intention, create a foundation for nurturing a deeper connection to yourself.*

### 6. Reflect and Adapt

- After completing your ritual, take a few moments to reflect on how it felt.
- Consider keeping a ritual journal to see what resonates and how the practice changes over time.
- Adjust your rituals to reflect your evolving needs and intentions.

### Ideas for Daily, Weekly, or Monthly Rituals

- **Daily:** Morning affirmations or gratitude journaling to start the day with positivity.
- **Weekly:** A Sunday ritual to reset and reflect on the week ahead.
- **Monthly:** A new moon or full moon ceremony to set intentions or release old energy.

### Tips for Sustaining Your Rituals

- **Keep It Simple:** Simplicity, particularly in everyday rituals, ensures consistency
- **Infuse Love:** Instead of striving for perfection, focus on joy and self-love.
- **Be Flexible:** Allow rituals to adjust to your schedule and energy levels.
- **Celebrate Your Commitment:** Acknowledge yourself for making time to honor your inner self.

### Incense suggestions based on intentions:

Including incense in your rituals is a lovely touch that elevates the sacred atmosphere and provides a sensory dimension of connection.

- **Sandalwood:** To promote grounding and spiritual connection.
- **Rose:** To invite love and compassion.
- **Frankincense:** For clarity, purification, and divine connection.
- **Cedar or Palo Santo:** To cleanse energy and create a protective space.
- **Myrrh:** To connect with ancient wisdom and inner stillness.

Pairing the aromas with your selected ritual stages will enhance the overall experience.

# Incense, Candles, Crystal, Roses for Self-Healing

## Incenses, Purposes, and Suggested Rituals

# INCENSES AND THEIR PURPOSES FOR CLEANSING AND HEALING

Different varieties of incense and their purposes, so you can choose the one that resonates with your ritual intention.

## Sage (White Sage)

- **Purpose:** Purification, clearing negative energy, protection
- **Ideal For:** Releasing past emotional baggage, creating a sacred space, protecting your energy.
- **Affirmation:** "I clear this space of all negativity, inviting light and positive energy into my life."

**Suggested Rituals:**
- **Space Clearing:** Use Sage before any ritual to cleanse your space from negative or stagnant energy, especially if you're starting a new chapter in life.
- **Personal Cleansing:** Wave the smoke around your body to release emotional baggage, stress, or negativity from past experiences.
- **Before Meditation or Prayer:** Purify the space and your energy to create a sacred atmosphere for spiritual practices.

## Palo Santo

- **Purpose:** Spiritual purification, grounding, calming
- **Ideal For:** Centering yourself, calming anxiety, and enhancing mindfulness.
- **Affirmation:** "I cleanse my space and mind, bringing peace and harmony into my being."

**Suggested Rituals:**
- **Calming and Centering:** Use Palo Santo when you feel scattered, stressed, or overwhelmed. Light it before journaling, meditation, or deep reflection to regain focus.
- **Emotional Healing:** Use it during moments of emotional healing, especially when dealing with grief, loss, or trauma. Its calming energy helps soothe and release emotional blocks.
- **Before Sleep:** Burn Palo Santo in the evening to promote restful sleep and remove any lingering energy that may disrupt your peace.

## Lavender

- **Purpose:** Relaxation, healing, stress relief
- **Ideal For:** Releasing tension, calming the mind, and inviting healing energy.
- **Affirmation:** "I release tension and invite peace and healing into my heart and soul."

**Suggested Rituals:**
- **Stress Relief:** Use Lavender after a long day to unwind. Light it while you take a warm bath or prepare for a restful sleep.
- **Emotional Balance:** Burn it during times of anxiety or emotional instability to help release tension and restore emotional peace.
- **For Self-Love Practices:** Burn Lavender before you do anything to nurture yourself—whether it's a self-care ritual, meditation, or simply sitting with yourself in stillness.

## Sandalwood

- **Purpose:** Clarity, spiritual awareness, grounding
- **Ideal For:** Deepening spiritual practices, enhancing focus, and clearing mental fog.
- **Affirmation:** "I invite clarity and spiritual connection, allowing my true self to emerge."

**Suggested Rituals:**
- **Meditation and Prayer:** Use Sandalwood to deepen your meditation practice and invite clarity during spiritual reflection. Its calming yet grounding properties help you stay focused and present.
- **Manifestation Rituals:** If you're working on manifesting your goals or intentions, burn Sandalwood to encourage mental clarity and spiritual connection.
- **Daily Grounding:** Use it when you need to reconnect with your body, stay grounded, and release any feelings of being "unbalanced."

# INCENSES AND THEIR PURPOSES FOR CLEANSING AND HEALING

Different varieties of incense and their purposes, so you can choose the one that resonates with your ritual intention.

### Frankincense

- **Purpose:** Spiritual elevation, meditation, protection
- **Ideal For:** Connecting with your higher self, deepening meditation, and creating a sacred atmosphere.
- **Affirmation:** "I elevate my energy to the highest frequency of love and light."

**Suggested Rituals:**
- **Deep Meditation:** Light Frankincense before a meditation session to deepen the connection to your higher self and to elevate your spiritual awareness.
- **Protection:** Use Frankincense for protection, especially if you're working in an environment or space where energy feels heavy or unsafe.
- **Purifying Space:** Burn Frankincense when you want to purify your space before working on personal growth or spiritual practices.

### Rose

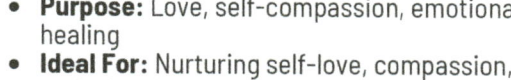

- **Purpose:** Love, self-compassion, emotional healing
- **Ideal For:** Nurturing self-love, compassion, and releasing emotional blockages.
- **Affirmation:** "I release any past hurts and embrace myself with love and compassion."

**Suggested Rituals:**
- **Self-Love Rituals:** Use Rose when you're doing inner work to nurture self-love and acceptance. Light it while doing mirror work, writing love letters to yourself, or any practice that cultivates self-compassion.
- **Emotional Healing:** Burn Rose incense after a difficult emotional experience to release pain and invite healing and emotional balance.
- **Heart-Centered Work:** Light it during journaling or meditations focused on heart-opening, forgiveness, and compassion.

### Cedarwood

- **Purpose:** Grounding, stability, protection
- **Ideal For:** Bringing a sense of calm and stability, protecting your personal space.
- **Affirmation:** "I am grounded and stable, rooted in my true self and protected from negativity."

**Suggested Rituals:**

- **Grounding Meditation:** Use Cedarwood before a grounding or root chakra meditation to create stability, both mentally and physically.
- **Protection:** Light it when you feel the need for protection or emotional boundaries, such as after a draining social interaction or before a major life decision.
- **Clearing Space for New Beginnings:** Burn Cedarwood when you're preparing to release something old and welcome something new in your life.

### Jasmine

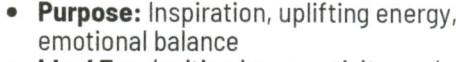
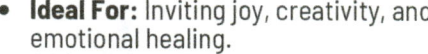

- **Purpose:** Inspiration, uplifting energy, emotional balance
- **Ideal For:** Inviting joy, creativity, and emotional healing.
- **Affirmation:** "I open my heart to joy, creativity, and uplifting energy."

**Suggested Rituals:**

- **Creative Energy:** Use Jasmine when you want to spark creativity, inspiration, or when working on creative projects, especially when feeling blocked.
- **Joyful Connection:** Burn Jasmine when you're engaging in joyful activities, such as a gathering with loved ones or during moments of gratitude and celebration.
- **Emotional Healing:** Light it to uplift your spirits during times of sadness, loneliness, or after experiencing emotional turbulence.

# INCENSES AND THEIR PURPOSES FOR CLEANSING AND HEALING

Different varieties of incense and their purposes, so you can choose the one that resonates with your ritual intention.

## Myrrh

- **Purpose:** Healing, purification, deep spiritual connection
- **Ideal For:** Deepening self-reflection, enhancing spiritual practices, and emotional healing.
- **Affirmation:** "I purify my energy and connect deeply with my true essence."

**Suggested Rituals:**
- **Healing Rituals:** Burn Myrrh when you're healing from deep emotional wounds, or when you're working through grief, trauma, or personal transformation.
- **Spiritual Reflection:** Use Myrrh for connecting to your higher self or during moments of quiet introspection and soul searching.
- **Purification:** Light Myrrh before embarking on any significant spiritual work or to purify your energy when you feel clouded or unclear.

## Cinnamon

- **Purpose:** Passion, energy, abundance
- **Ideal For:** Inviting vitality, passion, and abundance into your life.
- **Affirmation:** "I release all that blocks my abundance, welcoming passion, vitality, and success."

**Suggested Rituals:**
- **Manifesting Abundance:** Use Cinnamon to attract abundance and prosperity into your life, especially when working on financial goals, career development, or personal growth.
- **Inviting Passion:** Light it before engaging in any activity where you need to feel energized and motivated, such as exercise, creative pursuits, or setting new intentions.
- **Energy Boost:** Burn Cinnamon when you need an energetic boost or when you feel tired or uninspired.

## WHEN TO USE THESE INCENSES TOGETHER:

**For Deepening Meditation:** Frankincense, Palo Santo, Myrrh

**For Emotional Healing:** Lavender, Rose, Jasmine

**For Grounding & Protection:** Cedarwood, Sage

**For Inviting Abundance:** Cinnamon

**For Peace:** Sandalwood, Frankincense, Lavender, Blue Lotus, Cedar

**For Spiritual Clarity:** Sandalwood, Frankincense, Palo Santo

Page 110

# Daily Ritual Using Incenses

Incorporating these incenses into regular practices. These techniques can help you create a sacred space, promote personal growth, and deepen your spiritual or self-care routines:

**Morning Grounding Ritual (Start Your Day with Intention)**
**Incenses:** Palo Santo, Cedarwood, Sandalwood
- **Purpose:** Ground your energy, set a clear intention for the day, and create a peaceful, centered mind.
  **How to Use:**
  - Light Palo Santo or Cedarwood to purify the space and ground your energy.
  - As you breathe in the aroma, set an intention for the day. Think of what you wish to focus on or manifest, whether it's clarity, protection, or self-love.
  - Place the incense in a holder near where you'll meditate or journal.
  - Take a few deep breaths, feel the grounding energy, and say: *"I am grounded in the present moment. Today, I move with purpose and clarity."*

**Self-Love and Nurturing Ritual (Love Your Inner Being)**
**Incenses:** Rose, Lavender, Jasmine
- **Purpose:** Cultivate a sense of self-love, inner peace, and emotional balance.
  **How to Use:**
  - Light Rose or Lavender incense to create a soothing, loving atmosphere.
  - You can use this incense before your self-care routine, a nourishing bath, or a gentle face mask.
  - Set the intention to honor yourself, your needs, and your emotions.
  - Engage in activities that feel nurturing, like journaling, stretching, or simply sitting in stillness.
  - **Affirm:** *"I am worthy of love, peace, and compassion. I honor and nurture myself."*

**Meditation & Spiritual Clarity Ritual (Connect with Your Higher Self)**
**Incenses:** Frankincense, Sandalwood, Myrrh
- **Purpose:** Deepen spiritual connection, focus, and clarity during meditation.
  **How to Use:**
  - Light Frankincense or Sandalwood to elevate your space before meditation or prayer.
  - Close your eyes and focus on your breath, allowing the fragrance to guide your focus and heighten your spiritual awareness.
  - Sit in a comfortable position, and with each breath, feel your connection to your higher self growing stronger.
  - If using Myrrh, hold a crystal or sacred object and focus on it during your meditation to connect deeply with its energy.
  - **Affirm:** *"I am open to divine wisdom, clarity, and spiritual growth. I trust the guidance of my higher self."*

**Emotional Release & Healing Ritual (Let Go of Emotional Baggage)**
**Incenses:** Lavender, Rose, Sage
- **Purpose:** Release emotional baggage, heal old wounds, and invite emotional balance.
  **How to Use:**
  - Begin by lighting Sage to cleanse the space of negative or stagnant energy.
  - As the Sage burns, sit quietly, breathing deeply and releasing all tension.
  - Once the room feels clear, light Rose or Lavender incense to fill the space with soothing, healing energy.
  - Reflect on any emotions or memories that need releasing. Visualize these emotions leaving your body as you breathe.
  - **Affirm:** *"I release all emotional burdens and invite peace, healing, and love into my heart."*

# Daily Ritual Using Incenses

Incorporating these incenses into regular practices. These techniques can help you create a sacred space, promote personal growth, and deepen your spiritual or self-care routines:

### Manifestation Ritual (Attract Abundance and Success)
**Incenses:** Cinnamon, Sandalwood, Jasmine
- **Purpose:** Attract abundance, success, and inspiration into your life.

**How to Use:**
- Light Cinnamon incense to ignite passion and manifest your desires.
- Take a moment to set clear goals, whether they relate to personal growth, career, or relationships.
- Visualize your intentions as already manifesting, and feel gratitude for what is coming into your life.
- Use Jasmine to uplift your spirit and increase creative flow if you're working on artistic or professional projects.
- **Affirm:** *"I am open to receiving abundance and success. My heart and mind are aligned with my highest purpose."*

### Evening Relaxation Ritual (Release Tension and Prepare for Restful Sleep)
**Incenses:** Lavender, Palo Santo, Rose
- **Purpose:** Calm the mind, ease stress, and prepare for a restful night.

**How to Use:**
- Light Lavender incense to soothe the nervous system, relax the body, and calm the mind.
- Place it in your bedroom or near your meditation space as you begin your evening wind-down routine.
- Engage in relaxation practices such as gentle stretching, reading, or reflecting on gratitude for the day.
- If you want to invite loving energy before sleep, light Rose incense and focus on the love and peace surrounding you.
- **Affirm:** *"I release the stresses of the day. I am safe, peaceful, and ready for restful sleep."*

### Protection Ritual (Shield Yourself from Negative Energy)
**Incenses:** Palo Santo, Sage, Cedarwood
- **Purpose:** Protect your space and aura from negative influences.

**How to Use:**
- Light Sage or Palo Santo before any important meeting, travel, or when entering a new environment.
- Walk around your space, waving the incense smoke into corners, doorways, and windows to clear away negativity and protect the space.
- Focus on your intention to shield yourself from external negativity.
- **Affirm:** *"I am protected from negativity, and I trust my inner strength to guide me."*

### Creative Spark Ritual (Inspire Passion and Creativity)
**Incenses:** Jasmine, Cinnamon, Sandalwood
- **Purpose:** Ignite inspiration and flow during creative pursuits.

**How to Use:**
- Light Cinnamon or Jasmine incense to stimulate creativity and inspire new ideas.
- Use this ritual before starting work on artistic projects, writing, or any endeavor that requires creative flow.
- Set a clear intention for creativity and allow the fragrance to guide your focus.
- **Affirm:** *"I am a vessel for creativity and inspiration. My ideas flow freely and effortlessly."*

# ROSES AND THEIR SYMBOLISM FOR HEALING

Roses are extremely symbolic and have a powerful energy, making them suitable for rituals or practices that promote celibacy, self-love, and sacred intentions.

### White Roses: Purity and Sacred Intentions

**Symbolism:** Represent purity, spiritual love, and devotion to higher principles. They align with the commitment to celibacy as a sacred practice.

**Ritual Use:**
- Place white roses in your space during meditation to invoke purity of thought and intention.
- Use white rose petals in a cleansing bath to symbolize releasing attachments and connecting to divine energy.
- Offer a white rose as an altar centerpiece to honor your commitment to self-love and spiritual growth.

### Pink Roses: Gentle Self-Love and Nurturing

**Symbolism:** Represent love, compassion, and emotional healing, encouraging you to nurture yourself with grace and tenderness.

**Ritual Use:**
- Scatter pink rose petals around your journal as you write affirmations of self-worth and gratitude.
- Infuse rose petals into oils or teas to create nurturing self-care practices.
- Incorporate pink roses into visualization exercises to reinforce gentle self-love and emotional renewal.

### Red Roses: Inner Passion and Commitment

**Symbolism:** Often associated with romantic love, red roses can also symbolize a passionate commitment to your path and inner strength.

**Ritual Use:**
- Use a single red rose to honor your inner fire, channeling the energy of passion into creative and spiritual pursuits.
- Add red rose petals to rituals where you declare your devotion to self-mastery and transformation.

## RITUAL IDEAS WITH ROSES FOR CELIBACY

**Morning Devotion Ritual:**
- Begin your day by placing a rose on your bedside table or altar.
- Focus on its beauty and set an intention for the day, such as *"I honor myself and my sacred path."*
- Hold the rose and repeat a personal affirmation or prayer.

**Rose Water Blessing:**

- Create rose water by steeping rose petals in distilled water.
- Use the rose water to anoint yourself before meditation or journaling, symbolizing spiritual cleansing and self-renewal.

# ROSES AND THEIR SYMBOLISM FOR HEALING

Roses are extremely symbolic and have a powerful energy, making them suitable for rituals or practices that promote celibacy, self-love, and sacred intentions.

### Candle and Rose Ceremony:
- Light a white candle surrounded by rose petals.
- Meditate on the flame, envisioning it cleansing and strengthening your resolve for celibacy and self-love.
- Close the ritual by holding a rose to your heart and offering gratitude to yourself.

### Full Moon Rose Bath:
- During a full moon, draw a bath and add rose petals (white for purity, pink for self-love, or a mix).
- As you soak, release any lingering energy that no longer serves you and embrace the sacredness of your chosen path.

## ROSE OILS AND SCENTS

Rose essential oil or rose incense can enhance your rituals. These scents are known to improve mood, promote calm within, and open the heart chakra. Use them before journaling or during meditation.

## VISUALIZATION WITH ROSES

- Imagine holding a blooming rose in your heart center.
- Visualize its petals opening, radiating love and light through your entire being.
- Let it represent the beauty and sacredness within you.

# PAIRING INCENSE WITH CRYSTALS

Combining incense with crystals is an effective technique to enhance intentions, create harmony, and intensify the energy of ceremonies. Here's how to match various incenses with crystals depending on their complementary energies:

## Peace and Tranquility

- **Incense:** Lavender or Sandalwood
- **Crystals:** Amethyst, Selenite, Blue Lace Agate
- **Why:** Lavender and sandalwood calm the mind, and these crystals enhance serenity and relaxation.
- **Affirmation:** *"I embrace the calm within me, releasing all worries as I align with peace."*

## Self-Love and Compassion

- **Incense:** Rose or Jasmine
- **Crystals:** Rose Quartz, Rhodonite, Morganite
- **Why:** Rose and jasmine nurture the heart, and these crystals radiate love and emotional healing.
- **Affirmation:** *"I honor myself with love and compassion, knowing I am worthy of all goodness."*

## Grounding and Stability

- **Incense:** Frankincense or Cedarwood
- **Crystals:** Smoky Quartz, Hematite, Black Tourmaline
- **Why:** Frankincense and cedarwood connect to the earth, while these crystals anchor and stabilize energy.
- **Affirmation:** *"I am rooted in the present moment, balanced, and supported by the Earth."*

## Spiritual Growth and Intuition

- **Incense:** Myrrh or Palo Santo
- **Crystals:** Lapis Lazuli, Labradorite, Clear Quartz
- **Why:** Myrrh and Palo Santo open spiritual pathways, while these crystals enhance intuition and wisdom.
- **Affirmation:** *"I trust my inner wisdom and allow divine guidance to flow through me."*

## Cleansing and Renewal

- **Incense:** White Sage or Eucalyptus
- **Crystals:** Clear Quartz, Citrine, Fluorite
- **Why:** These incense types and crystals purify energy, clearing blockages for a fresh start.
- **Affirmation:** *"I release what no longer serves me and welcome a fresh, vibrant energy into my life."*

## Protection and Strength

- **Incense:** Dragon's Blood or Patchouli
- **Crystals:** Obsidian, Garnet, Tiger's Eye
- **Why:** Dragon's Blood and Patchouli create a protective shield, complemented by these empowering crystals.
- **Affirmation:** *"I am surrounded by a shield of light, safe, and empowered in all that I do."*

## Creativity and Inspiration

- **Incense:** Orange Blossom or Cinnamon
- **Crystals:** Carnelian, Sunstone, Citrine
- **Why:** These combinations boost motivation, creativity, and joy.
- **Affirmation:** *"My creative energy flows freely, and I bring my ideas to life with joy."*

## Love and Passion

- **Incense:** Ylang Ylang or Sandalwood
- **Crystals:** Garnet, Ruby, Rose Quartz
- **Why:** These incense types stimulate passion, and the crystals support love and connection.
- **Affirmation:** *"I radiate love and passion, deepening my connection with myself and others."*

## Healing and Emotional Release

- **Incense:** Chamomile or Vanilla
- **Crystals:** Lepidolite, Amazonite, Moonstone
- **Why:** Chamomile and vanilla soothe emotions, while these crystals support deep healing.
- **Affirmation:** *"I release past pain and embrace healing as I grow into my highest self."*

## Manifestation and Abundance

- **Incense:** Cinnamon or Bay Leaf
- **Crystals:** Pyrite, Green Aventurine, Citrine
- **Why:** These incense types and crystals attract prosperity and amplify manifestation energy.
- **Affirmation:** *"Abundance flows into my life effortlessly, and I welcome it with gratitude."*

# PAIRING INCENSE WITH CRYSTALS

Combining incense with crystals is an effective technique to enhance intentions, create harmony, and intensify the energy of ceremonies. Here's how to match various incenses with crystals depending on their complementary energies:

## USING THIS IN RITUAL

- **Preparation:** Light the incense and cleanse the crystal with its smoke.
- **Focus:** Hold the crystal while repeating the affirmation three times.
- **Meditation:** Sit with the incense and crystal, visualizing their combined energy infusing your intention.
- **Close:** Thank the incense and crystal for their support, and place the crystal in a sacred space to continue working with your intention.

## TIPS FOR PAIRING

- **Set Intentions:** Choose the pair based on your goal for the ritual (peace, healing, manifestation, etc.).
- **Placement:** Place the crystal near the incense burner or hold it while the incense burns.
- **Combine Energies:** Visualize the crystal absorbing the incense's energy, amplifying your intention.
- **Cycle of Use:** Cleanse your crystals with the incense smoke before or after pairing to maintain purity.

# CHOOSING CANDLE COLORS AND THEIR MEANINGS

Candles have the unique ability to create a relaxing environment, focus your intention, and magnify your rituals. Each candle color represents a distinct energy that can help you achieve your goals and strengthen your connection to yourself. Candles combined with affirmations help you realize your intentions with greater clarity and purpose.

### White (Purity, Clarity, and Peace)

- **Meaning:** Symbolizes purity, spiritual connection, and the clearing of negative energies.
- **Affirmation:** *"I release what no longer serves me and invite clarity and peace into my life."*

### Pink (Love, Compassion, and Emotional Healing)

- **Meaning:** Represents unconditional love, self-care, and emotional balance.
- **Affirmation:** *"I am worthy of infinite love, and I nurture my heart with compassion."*

### Red (Passion, Strength, and Vitality)

- **Meaning:** Embodies energy, courage, and a grounding connection to life.
- **Affirmation:** *"I honor my strength and embrace my inner power with boldness."*

### Orange (Creativity, Joy, and Optimism)

- **Meaning:** Sparks enthusiasm, creativity, and a zest for life.
- **Affirmation:** *"I radiate joy and allow my creativity to flow effortlessly."*

### Yellow (Confidence, Happiness, and Mental Clarity)

- **Meaning:** Reflects positivity, self-confidence, and intellectual focus.
- **Affirmation:** *"I shine brightly with confidence, illuminating my path with joy."*

### Green (Growth, Healing, and Abundance)

- **Meaning:** Represents renewal, balance, and prosperity.
- **Affirmation:** *"I grow with grace and welcome abundance in every form."*

### Blue (Calm, Communication, and Inner Peace)

- **Meaning:** Enhances tranquility, intuition, and honest self-expression.
- **Affirmation:** *"I communicate my truth with ease and rest in inner peace."*

### Purple (Spirituality, Wisdom, and Intuition)

- **Meaning:** Encourages deeper insight, spiritual growth, and inner wisdom.
- **Affirmation:** *"I trust my intuition and embrace the wisdom within me."*

### Black (Protection, Release, and Transformation)

- **Meaning:** Provides grounding, shields from negativity, and supports letting go.
- **Affirmation:** *"I am safe and protected as I transform into my highest self."*

### Gold (Success, Prosperity, and Divine Guidance)

- **Meaning:** Symbolizes achievement, divine blessings, and abundance.
- **Affirmation:** *"I am aligned with the flow of divine prosperity and success."*

# CHOOSING CANDLE COLORS AND THEIR MEANINGS

Candles have the unique ability to create a relaxing environment, focus your intention, and magnify your rituals. Each candle color represents a distinct energy that can help you achieve your goals and strengthen your connection to yourself. Candles combined with affirmations help you realize your intentions with greater clarity and purpose.

## INCORPORATING CANDLES INTO RITUALS

1. **Set the Scene:** Place your chosen candle in a quiet, clean, and sacred space. Surround it with items that inspire connection, such as crystals, fresh flowers, or meaningful objects.

2. **Infuse with Intention:** Before lighting, hold the candle and speak your affirmation aloud. Visualize the flame carrying your intentions into the universe.

3. **Light the Candle with Purpose:** As the flame ignites, imagine your desires of affirmations taking form. Feel the energy of the color and affirmation enveloping you.

4. **Pair with Practices:**

- During meditation, let the candle's light be your focus, grounding your thoughts.

- In journaling, write by the glow of a color that resonates with your intention.

- For mirror work, gaze into the candle's flame as you recite affirmations to enhance self-connection.

5. **Release and Gratitude:** Once your ritual feels complete, extinguish the candle with gratitude. Reflect on the energy you've invited into your life.

## TIPS FOR CANDLE SAFETY AND SACRED USE

- Use natural, non-toxic candles like soy or beeswax for a pure experience.

- Place candles on a fireproof surface, away from flammable items.

- Never leave candles unattended or within reach of children or pets.

# CREATING YOUR SACRED ALTAR

An altar is a physical reflection of your inner connection, as well as a dedicated space for honoring your rituals and intentions. Setting up an altar brings tranquility, mindfulness, and sacred energy into your space.

### Choose a Space

Select a quiet, uncluttered area in your home where you can focus without distractions. It could be a table, a shelf, or even a small corner dedicated solely to your altar.

### Cleanse the Space

Use incense, sage, palo santo, or sound bowls to energetically clear the space before arranging your items. This ensures your altar begins with fresh, positive energy.

### Incorporate Sacred Elements

Include elements that resonate with your spiritual practice:

- **Candles:** Representing light, clarity, and transformation (refer back to your candle section for color meanings).
- **Crystals:** Symbolizing grounding, love, or clarity (paired with the energy of your chosen ritual).
- **Flowers or Plants:** To symbolize growth, beauty, and connection with nature.
- **Sacred Symbols:** Such as the Ankh, mandalas, or anything meaningful to your spiritual journey.
- **Offerings:** Place offerings like fruit, herbs, or water to honor your intentions or spiritual guides.

### Personal Touches

- Add photos, affirmations, or mementos that inspire and uplift you.
- Include a journal or small notebook for reflections or writing intentions.
- Use fabrics, such as silk or natural cloth, to create a base for your altar that feels soft and sacred.

### Intentional Arrangement

Arrange your altar pieces with mindfully, focusing on balance and harmony. Consider a central focal point, such as a candle or sacred symbol, from which items radiate outward.

### Set an Intention

Before using your altar, set an intention. Speak it out or in your heart to fill the area with your energy and purpose.

# CREATING YOUR SACRED ALTAR

An altar is a physical reflection of your inner connection, as well as a dedicated space for honoring your rituals and intentions. Setting up an altar brings tranquility, mindfulness, and sacred energy into your space.

**Altar Ritual Ideas**

- Light candles and meditate in front of your altar to connect with your inner self.
- Use the space for journaling, affirmations, or gratitude practice.
- Refresh your altar regularly by cleansing it and rotating items based on your current intentions or seasonal shifts.

**Affirmation for Setting Your Altar:**

*"This sacred space reflects my inner truth, love, and light.*

*Here, I honor my connection to myself and the universe.*

*I invite peace, wisdom, and divine energy into my life."*

# CHAPTER 04

> Celibacy isn't about restriction; it's about liberation. It's a conscious decision to redirect energy often dispersed outward back into yourself, creating a sanctuary of empowerment. It increases clarity, intuition, and a stronger connection to your inner wisdom and the divine.

**@ Empress Nefertiti-Mumbi**

# CELIBACY AS SACRED SELF-LOVE:

## TRANSMUTING ENERGY INTO DIVINE CREATIVITY

THE SACREDNESS OF SELF-LOVE

# Table of Contents

## 01 — Page 125
### BENEFITS OF CELIBACY
Physical energy, emotional harmony, spiritual development, and improved concentration.

## 02 — Page 131
### THE SPIRITUAL ASPECT
How celibacy aligns your energy with higher vibrations, promoting calm, clarity, and divine connection.

## 03 — Page 142
### ENERGY TRANSMUTATION
Transforming sexual energy into creative energy that fuels art, purpose, and meaningful pursuits.

## 04 — Page 148
### SELF-LOVE AND EMPOWERMENT
Nurturing self-worth involves prioritizing healing and joy, so deepening your sense of wholeness.

## 05 — Page 164
### CELIBACY, DECLARATION, ANNIVERSARY & AFFIRMATION
Honor and celebrate the annual journey of self-love, spiritual growth, and empowerment

# Celibacy as Sacred Self-Love: Transmuting Energy into Divine Creativity

This chapter dives into the profound journey of celibacy as a form of self-love and spiritual discipline. It explores the advantages of choosing celibacy not as deprivation, but as an intentional decision to honor your spiritual essence. By embracing celibacy, you create place for healing, clarity, and a strong connection with your inner self.

**The chapter will highlight:**

**Benefits of Celibacy:** Physical energy, emotional harmony, spiritual development, and improved concentration.
- **The Essence of Celibacy:** Why celibacy is more than abstinence—it's a spiritual declaration of self-worth.
- **The Physical and Emotional Benefits:** Improved energy, focus, and inner peace.

**The Spiritual Aspect:** How celibacy aligns your energy with higher vibrations, promoting calm, clarity, and divine connection.
- **Celibacy and Spiritual Growth:** How celibacy connects you with the divine and strengthens your intuition.

**Energy Transmutation:** Transforming sexual energy into creative energy that fuels art, purpose, and meaningful pursuits.
- **Transmutation Practices:** Techniques to channel energy into creative outlets (e.g., journaling, art, meditation).

**Self-Love and Empowerment:** Nurturing self-worth involves prioritizing healing and joy, so deepening your sense of wholeness.
- **Daily Practices for Sacred Celibacy:** Creating rituals and routines to keep your commitment.
- Affirmations for Empowerment: Words that empower, inspire, and center yourself in love.

# BENEFITS OF CELIBACY

Physical energy, emotional harmony, spiritual development, and improved concentration.

## The Essence of Celibacy

Celibacy is a profound choice that transcends the notion of mere abstinence. At its root, it is a sacred act of recognizing oneself as a channel of divine energy, love, and creativity. By committing to celibacy, you align with a higher vibration of self-awareness and self-respect, allowing your energy to flow inward for healing, growth, and transformation.

Celibacy isn't about restriction; it's about liberation. It's a conscious decision to redirect energy often dispersed outward back into yourself, creating a sanctuary of empowerment. It increases clarity, intuition, and a stronger connection to your inner wisdom and the divine.

Celibacy acknowledges your sacredness, admiring your body and energies as gifts to be treasured and nurtured. This path encourages you to see love, intimacy, and connection through a holistic lens—one that starts with a deeply rooted love for yourself.

**Key Principles of Celibacy as a Sacred Choice**

**1. Reclaiming Your Energy**
- Celibacy allows you to conserve and redirect your sexual energy, also known as prana. This potent force, when harnessed, nourishes your creativity, spirituality, and overall vitality.
- Envision it like caring for a bright spark within, fanning it into a radiant flame that illuminates your path.

**2. Deepening Self-Love**
- By choosing celibacy, you commit to prioritizing your personal well-being and inner peace
- It strengthens introspection and self-awareness, leading you to find what actually nourishes your soul.

**3. Spiritual Alignment**
- Many spiritual traditions embrace celibacy as a means to enlightenment. It eliminates distractions and creates pathways for greater consciousness, inner serenity, and spiritual connection.
- Celibacy teaches patience and the beauty of delayed gratification, keeping you grounded in the present now.

# BENEFITS OF CELIBACY

Physical energy, emotional harmony, spiritual development, and improved concentration.

## The Essence of Celibacy

**4. Sacred Empowerment**
- Celibacy empowers you to uphold your boundaries and create relationships centered on respect, love, and shared values.
- It allows you to define intimacy in your own terms, emphasizing emotional, spiritual, and intellectual connections.

**5. Deepening Self-Love**
- By choosing celibacy, you commit to prioritizing your personal well-being and inner peace
- It strengthens introspection and self-awareness, leading you to find what actually nourishes your soul.

**6. Transmuting Energy**
- Celibacy transmits sexual energy into useful and gratifying activities through mindfulness, meditation, and creative practices.

## Reflective Questions for Journaling

1. What does celibacy mean to me, and why am I choosing this path?

2. How can I use celibacy to deepen my relationship with myself and the divine?

3. In what ways can I channel my sexual energy into creative or spiritual pursuits?

4. What boundaries or practices can I establish to honor my commitment to celibacy?

5. How does embracing celibacy make me feel about my body, mind, and spirit?

# Affirmation Practice for Embracing the Essence of Celibacy

Stand in front of a mirror and repeat these affirmations daily:

I am sacred, whole, and worthy of love in all its forms.

I honor my energy and channel it into my growth and creativity.

My choice to embrace celibacy empowers and uplifts me.

I am in harmony with myself and aligned with the divine within.

Celibacy is a gift I give to myself; it nurtures my soul and strengthens my spirit.

# BENEFITS OF CELIBACY

Physical energy, emotional harmony, spiritual development, and improved concentration.

## The Physical and Emotional Benefits of Celibacy

Celibacy is more than just a spiritual or philosophical commitment; it also has significant physical and emotional advantages that nourish the mind, body, and soul. By consciously choosing celibacy, you allow your life force energy to be redirected within, resulting in regeneration, clarity, and a greater sense of calm.

## Physical Benefits

**1. Improved Energy and Vitality**

- Sexual energy is a potent life force that, when conserved and transmuted, fuels the body's physical and creative energy.
- Many people report feeling more alive and invigorated as their bodies use this energy to heal and revitalize themselves.
- The conserved energy can be directed toward activities that need concentration and stamina, such as exercise, artistic hobbies, or spiritual practices.

**2. Enhanced Focus and Mental Clarity**

- Celibacy reduces distractions and increases your capacity to concentrate.
- By avoiding the emotional and hormonal changes that are common in sexual relationships, you can establish a mental environment that promotes productivity and self-reflection.
- It increases better decision-making and the ability to be present in your regular activities.

**3. Better Physical Health**

- Choosing celibacy can reduce stress and physical strain, resulting in better sleep and overall well-being.
- It can also help with hormone balance and give the body time to heal itself without external emotional stresses or attachments.

# BENEFITS OF CELIBACY

Physical energy, emotional harmony, spiritual development, and improved concentration.

## The Physical and Emotional Benefits of Celibacy

Celibacy is more than just a spiritual or philosophical commitment; it also has significant physical and emotional advantages that nourish the mind, body, and soul. By consciously choosing celibacy, you allow your life force energy to be redirected within, resulting in regeneration, clarity, and a greater sense of calm.

## Emotional Benefits

### 1. Inner Peace and Stability

- Celibacy gives emotional stability by eliminating the problems associated with physical connections.
- It promotes self-reflection and healing from past emotional wounds, which aids in the development of inner peace.

### 2. Strengthened Self-Worth

- By choosing celibacy, you reinforce the belief that your value is inherent and not reliant on external validation.
- This sense of self-worth promotes more confidence and self-esteem.

### 3. Emotional Freedom

- Celibacy removes the emotional highs and lows which often accompany romantic relationships, helping you to stay balanced.
- This freedom empowers you to explore and grow your emotional intelligence, which improves your ability to navigate relationships and encounters.

### 4. Heightened Emotional Awareness

- With fewer distractions, you become more attuned to your emotional surface
- Celibacy empowers you to recognize and confront underlying emotions, which promotes growth in emotions and resilience.

# PRACTICAL APPLICATIONS
## FOR HARNESSING THESE BENEFITS

### Daily Meditation for Energy and Focus

Begin your day with a 10–15 minute meditation, visualizing your conserved energy glowing within you, radiating outward to fuel your tasks and goals.

### Journaling for Clarity and Emotional Awareness

Reflect daily on how celibacy has enhanced your ability to focus and maintain peace.

Use prompts such as, "What emotional patterns am I releasing today?" or "How has celibacy brought me closer to my true self?"

### Physical Practices for Vitality

Engage in grounding activities like yoga, tai chi, or nature walks to help circulate your conserved energy.

Practice mindful breathing exercises to boost your energy and maintain focus.

### Create Affirmations for Inner Peace and Confidence

Examples:

My energy flows within me, empowering every aspect of my life.

I am at peace with my choices and in harmony with myself.

I honor my body and emotions, cherishing the balance within.

# THE SPIRITUAL ASPECT
## Celibacy is The Purest Form of Love to Oneself

### Honoring the Sacred Vessel

Celibacy is more than just abstinence; it is a strong spiritual practice that transforms your inner energy into a divine connection. When you choose celibacy with intention, you open the way to a deeper relationship with your higher self, which brings clarity, tranquility, and a deep sense of purpose.

**Let's explore the key areas within this spiritual dimension:**

**1. Spiritual Renewal and Purification**

- **Detoxing Energetic Ties:** Every connection that you make leaves energetic imprints. Celibacy allows these imprints to vanish, restoring your vitality and replenishing your aura.
- **Sacred Reflection:** This activity invites you to consider your emotional and spiritual boundaries, releasing attachments that no longer serve your highest good.
- **Energetic Vibrancy:** With fewer distractions, you may find it simpler to elevate your spiritual vibration and connect with love, peace, and universal truths.

**Suggested Ritual:** Take a spiritual bath with sea salt, rose petals, and a few drops of lavender or frankincense oil. Light a white candle to symbolize purity and renewal, and meditate on the light filling your entire being.

**2. Harnessing Creative and Spiritual Energy**

- **Sacred Transmutation:** Celibacy saves energy, which is then transformed. You can use it for artistic endeavors, spiritual practices, or acts of service.
- **Heightened Intuition:** As your energy remains centered, your intuition improves, allowing you to place more trust in your inner voice.
- **Divine Feminine and Masculine Balance:** Celibacy promotes internal energy balance, aligning the sacred masculine structure with the divine feminine flow.

**Affirmation:** *"I am a vessel of divine creativity and spiritual purpose. I honor this sacred energy and channel it with love and intention."*

# THE SPIRITUAL ASPECT
## Celibacy is The Purest Form of Love to Oneself

## Honoring the Sacred Vessel

### 3. Connection to the Divine

- **Sacred Communion:** Celibacy may help you feel closer to the Divine Source and more aligned with universal love and wisdom.
- **Clarity of Spirit:** Without physical distractions, your spiritual practice grows deeper, and you may find it easier to connect through prayer, meditation, or nature walks.
- **Dreamwork and Intuition:** Celibacy can improve your dream life and intuitive insights since it reduces the amount of stimulation your mind and body get.

**Suggested Practice:** Dedicate a space in your home for spiritual connection, such as a small altar. Include items that resonate with your journey, like crystals (amethyst for spiritual clarity or clear quartz for focus), incense, and sacred symbols.

### 4. Embodying Sacred Wholeness

- **Self-Love as Devotion:** Celibacy allows you to experience yourself as whole and complete, realizing you are sacred and sufficient without external validation.
- **Divine Union Within:** By delving inside, you create a space for the divine union of your inner feminine and masculine energies, transforming yourself into your own love sanctuary.
- **Ritual of Gratitude:** Celebrate your wholeness every day by writing three things you're grateful for about your journey, including your body, mind, and spirit.

**Affirmation:** "I am whole, sacred, and loved. My energy flows with divine purpose and infinite light."

### 5. Sacred Commitment to Yourself

Celibacy is an act of dedication, not deprivation. It is a commitment that embraces your body as a temple, your mind as a garden, and your soul as an endless source of light. With one decision, you begin a sacred journey of empowerment, healing, and divine connection.

**The Sacredness of Self-Love**  **Chapter 04**

# THE SPIRITUAL ASPECT

Celibacy is The Purest Form of Love to Oneself

## Protecting Yourself Spiritually from Unwanted Energies: Emphasizing Awareness, Tools, and Affirmations:s

### 1. Understanding Spiritual Sovereignty

- **Acknowledging Your Power:** Recognize that you are the master of your energy. No entity or energy has authority over you unless you grant it.
- **The Power of Consent:** Energies often attempt to manipulate through vulnerability or permission (even unconscious). Declare No Consent and take back your power.
- **No Fear Approach:** Fear weakens your energetic defenses. Embrace courage by affirming your sacred nature.

### 2. Tools for Spiritual Protection

#### A. Setting Energetic Boundaries

- **Visualization Technique:** Imagine a radiant, impenetrable light surrounding your entire being. This can be a golden sphere, a crystalline shield, or a cocoon of white light.
- **Daily Intention Setting:** Begin each day by declaring, "I am surrounded by divine protection, and only energies aligned with my highest good may enter my field."

#### B. Protective Symbols and Talismans

- Use sacred symbols like the Ankh, Eye of Horus, or sacred geometry to reinforce your protection.
- Wear crystals like black tourmaline (grounding), amethyst (spiritual shielding), or selenite (purity and light).

#### C. Clearing and Cleansing Rituals

- **Smudging:** Use sage, palo santo, or frankincense to cleanse your space and aura regularly.
- **Salt Baths:** Soak in a bath with Epsom salt, Himalayan salt, and protective herbs like rosemary or lavender to release attachments.

# THE SPIRITUAL ASPECT

### Celibacy is The Purest Form of Love to Oneself

## Protecting Yourself Spiritually from Unwanted Energies: Emphasizing Awareness, Tools, and Affirmations:s

### D. Protection in the Dream State

- Set intentions before sleeping, declaring, *"I enter my dream space as a sovereign being, shielded by divine protection."*
- Place a piece of **amethyst** or **clear quartz** near your bed to enhance clarity and guard against intrusions.
- Consider wearing an **eye mask** or keeping protective symbols like a sigil under your pillow.

## Benefits of Wearing an Eye Mask

Using an eye mask in the dream state offers subtle yet deep benefits that can improve your spiritual and energetic protection:

### a. Blocking Out External Stimuli

An eye mask protects your eyes from light and distractions in your environment, resulting in a greater sense of serenity. This darkness encourages a more relaxed mood, making it simpler to enter a dream state in which you feel more in control and less influenced by outside forces.

### b. Fostering Inner Focus

By covering your eyes, the mask helps direct your attention inward, reducing distractions that could pull you out of alignment with your spiritual intentions. This internal attention improves your bond with your inner self and higher forces, offering a sense of security.

### c. Energetic Boundary

An eye mask serves as both a physical and symbolic barrier. In spiritual terms, it creates a delicate energetic shield around the windows of your soul (your eyes). This can keep undesirable energies from entering your subconscious via visual or energetic entrance points during vulnerable dream states.

# THE SPIRITUAL ASPECT

Celibacy is The Purest Form of Love to Oneself

## Protecting Yourself Spiritually from Unwanted Energies: Emphasizing Awareness, Tools, and Affirmations:s

### d. Enhancing Lucidity

An eye mask might create a sense of security, allowing you to have more clear dreams. When you feel safe, you are more likely to stay alert in your dreams, allowing you to actively declare your power, establish boundaries, and redirect any negative energy.

### e. Anchoring Ritual Intentions

When accompanied with affirmations or pre-sleep rituals, wearing an eye mask becomes a sacred gesture. It alerts your subconscious that you are entering a safe area where only energies aligned with your highest good are welcome.

**How to Use an Eye Mask for Spiritual Protection:**

- *Choose a Sacred Mask:* Choose an eye mask made from natural, breathable fabrics. You may even have one infused with a relaxing aroma like lavender or charged with crystals.

- *Set Your Intentions:* Before putting on the mask, declare your intent, such as:

*"As I wear this mask, I shield myself from all energies that do not serve my highest good."*

- *Visualize a Shield of Light:* Imagine a sphere of protective light around your entire being as you prepare for rest, with the mask acting as the final layer of this shield.

- *Cleanse Regularly:* Energetically cleanse your eye mask by placing it in sunlight, moonlight, or smudging with cleansing herbs like sage or palo santo.

# THE SPIRITUAL ASPECT

### Celibacy is The Purest Form of Love to Oneself

## Protecting Yourself Spiritually from Unwanted Energies: Emphasizing Awareness, Tools, and Affirmations:s

### 3. Affirmations for Protection

Here are affirmations designed to help you restore your spiritual authority and block negative energies:

- *I am a sovereign being, protected by divine light and unconditional love.*

- *No energy or entity has power over me without my consent.*

- *I declare my energy sacred and inviolate, shielded by my highest self.*

- *I transmute all unwanted energies into wisdom, growth, and peace.*

- *I command all energies not aligned with my highest good to return to the light, never to return for all eternity.*

- *I awaken in full awareness of my power and spiritual authority.*

### 4. Declaring and Commanding Energy

When you encounter unfavorable energy in your dream or waking state, consider the following technique.

- **Awaken and Anchor:** Focus on your breath and ground yourself, affirming, "I am fully awake and in control."
- **Declare Authority**: Firmly say, "I revoke all permissions, explicit or implicit, given to any entity, energy, or being to access my field. I am sovereign and free."
- **Send the Energy Away:** With intention, state, "I send all energies not serving my highest good to the light. You may not return to me in this or any lifetime for eternity."
- **Seal Your Space:** Visualize yourself in a shield of impenetrable light, sealing off any access points

# THE SPIRITUAL ASPECT
## Celibacy is The Purest Form of Love to Oneself

### Protecting Yourself Spiritually from Unwanted Energies: Emphasizing Awareness, Tools, and Affirmations:s

**5. Transmuting Energy into Wisdom**

Transmuting unwanted energy into something that serves you is a profound act of alchemy.

- **Invocation of Light:** Call upon divine energies (cosmic forces within, ancestors, or your higher self) to assist in transforming these experiences.
- **Journaling Exercise:** Reflect on the encounter. Ask, "What lesson or wisdom does this hold for my growth?"
- **Creative Expression:** Transform the energy into art, writing, or other creative outlets to reclaim it as your own.

**6. Ritual for Empowering Your Space and Energy**

This can be done after an encounter or as a regular practice:

- *Prepare the Space:* Light protective incense (e.g., frankincense or sandalwood) and a white candle.
- *Cleanse the Area:* Use a smudge stick or sound healing tools (like a bell or tuning fork) to clear stagnant energy.
- *Declare Your Sovereignty:* Speak aloud, "This space is sacred. I claim it as my sanctuary, protected and free from intrusion."
- *Invoke Support:* Call upon your spiritual guides or divine energies to assist in maintaining this protection.
- *Seal with Gratitude:* Close with, "I thank the universe for this sacred shield of love and light."

**The Sacredness of Self-Love**  Chapter 04

# THE SPIRITUAL ASPECT
### Celibacy is The Purest Form of Love to Oneself

## The Sacred Bridge Between the Physical and Cosmic Womb

**Write or reflect on the following:**

**1. Visualize the Connection:** Close your eyes and imagine your physical womb or womb space as a radiant vessel of light. See it as a sacred portal connected to the vast cosmic womb of creation. What sensations, emotions, or imagery arise as you bridge these two realms?

**2. Creative Power and Unity:** Reflect on how the energy of your physical womb mirrors the infinite creative potential of the cosmic womb. How does this connection inspire you in your daily life, your creative endeavors, and your relationships?

**3. Healing and Harmony:** Write about how aligning your womb space with the cosmic womb can bring healing, balance, and empowerment into your life. Are there specific moments when you've felt this sacred alignment?

**4. Sacred Rituals for Connection:** Imagine or describe rituals or practices that honor this connection, such as movement, meditation, or journaling. How do these practices deepen your awareness of your inner and universal creative power?

**5. Affirming the Connection:** Create affirmations that celebrate your unity with the cosmic womb.

**Examples include:**
- *"I am a sacred vessel of creation, connected to the infinite wisdom of the cosmos."*
- *"My womb is a divine portal of healing, love, and abundance."*
- *"Through my womb, I align with the eternal rhythms of the universe."*

**6. Gratitude and Offering:** End by writing a note of gratitude to your physical womb and the cosmic womb for their shared role in your life's journey. What do you wish to offer back to this sacred relationship as an act of devotion and love?

**Note: For visualization, consider the art piece on next page "The Sacred Bridge Between the Physical and Cosmic Womb".**

The Sacred Bridge Between the Physical and Cosmic Womb @Empress Nefertiti-Mumbi

# Exercise: WOMB AWAKENING AND CONNECTION

This exercise involves breathwork, visualization, movement, and affirmations to nurture and awaken the connection between your physical womb (or womb space) and the cosmic womb of creation.

## Elevate Your Well-being

### Preparation

**1. Create a Sacred Space**

- Light a non-toxic candle (consider red, orange, or gold for womb energy) and burn incense like myrrh, sandalwood, or frankincense.
- Place crystals such as carnelian, moonstone, or rose quartz nearby.
- Use a comfortable cushion, yoga mat, or chair in a quiet place where you won't be disturbed.

**2. Set Your Intention**

- Take a moment to declare your intention: *"I honor the sacred connection between my physical and cosmic womb. I awaken my creative and nurturing energy."*

### Steps

**1. Grounding Breathwork**

- Sit comfortably and place one hand over your heart and the other over your lower belly (womb space).
- Take deep breaths in through the nose, sending the breath into your lower belly. Feel it expand with each inhale.
- On the exhale, release any tension, visualizing stagnant energy leaving your womb.
- Repeat this for 5 minutes, allowing your body to relax and your energy to ground.

**2. Cosmic Womb Visualization**

- Close your eyes and imagine a glowing, warm light in your womb space.
- See this light as a golden or silver orb, representing your creative and nurturing energy.
- Now, visualize this orb expanding outward, connecting to the vast cosmic womb of the universe—a limitless field of creation and love.
- Feel the cosmic womb pouring healing, love, and wisdom back into your womb space, creating a continuous exchange of energy.

**3. Affirmation Integration**

As you visualize, speak these affirmations aloud or internally:

- *"I am connected to the sacred source of creation within me."*
- *"My womb is a portal of infinite wisdom, healing, and creativity."*
- *"I release all that does not serve my highest good, and I welcome pure energy of love and light."*
- *"I trust the divine power of my womb to guide and nurture me."*

# Exercise: WOMB AWAKENING AND CONNECTION

This exercise involves breathwork, visualization, movement, and affirmations to nurture and awaken the connection between your physical womb (or womb space) and the cosmic womb of creation.

## Elevate Your Well-being

**4. Movement for Activation**

- Begin gentle, circular movements of your hips, either seated or standing. This awakens the flow of energy in the sacral chakra and womb space.
- As you move, chant *"Aaaah"* (the sound frequency of creation) or sing tones that resonate with you.
- Feel the energy expand and flow freely through your body and into the cosmic womb connection.

**5. Closing the Practice**

- Place both hands over your womb and take three deep breaths.
- Whisper or think: *"I honor this sacred space as a vessel of creation and love. I am whole."*
- Blow out your candle with gratitude or extinguish it with a snuffer, closing the ritual with intention.

**Additional Practices to Strengthen Connection**

- **Journaling:** After your practice, write down any sensations, visions, or emotions you experienced. This helps deepen your awareness.
- **Sacred Baths:** Use herbs like basil, rose, or lavender, infused in warm water, to further cleanse and nourish your womb energy.
- **Daily Affirmation Ritual:** Stand in front of a mirror, place your hands on your womb, and repeat affirmations to reaffirm your connection.

# ENERGY TRANSMUTATION

Transforming sexual energy into creative energy
that fuels art, purpose, and meaningful pursuits.

## Transmuting Celibacy into Creativity: Suggestions for Creative Pursuits

Choosing celibacy empowers you to focus your energies on creative pursuits. This practice allows you to truly connect with your inner essence and express it externally through painting, writing, music, and other forms of creativity. Here are some ideas for using your conserved energy to cultivate creativity and self-expression.

### 1. Writing and Journaling

- **Autobiographical Writing:** Share your journey of celibacy, self-love, and healing in a blog, poetry, or even a book. Your story could inspire others to embark on their own path of self-discovery.
- **Daily Creative Journaling:** Use your journaling practice to explore new ideas or write affirmations, creating a repository of inspiration.
- **Storytelling:** Develop fictional tales rooted in themes of empowerment, balance, or spiritual growth.

### 2. Visual Art

- **Painting or Drawing:** Use your conserved energy to create art that reflects your emotions, dreams, and inner world. Experiment with colors that evoke love, peace, and vitality, like soft pinks, whites, and golds.
- **Mandala Creation:** Design intricate mandalas as a meditative practice, representing your journey and inner harmony.
- **Collage or Vision Boards:** Curate images and symbols that resonate with your goals, aspirations, and feelings of self-love.

### 3. Music and Movement

- **Create Music:** Compose melodies, chants, or songs that express your journey and inspire love and peace.
- **Dance as Creation:** Explore free-form dance or choreographed movement to connect with your body and release energy creatively.
- **Instrumental Expression:** If you play an instrument, experiment with creating uplifting or introspective pieces that reflect your emotions.

# ENERGY TRANSMUTATION

Transforming sexual energy into creative energy that fuels art, purpose, and meaningful pursuits.

## Transmuting Celibacy into Creativity: Suggestions for Creative Pursuits

Choosing celibacy empowers you to focus your energies on creative pursuits. This practice allows you to truly connect with your inner essence and express it externally through painting, writing, music, and other forms of creativity. Here are some ideas for using your conserved energy to cultivate creativity and self-expression.

### 4. Crafts and Handiwork

- **Candle Making:** Infuse candles with herbs and colors aligned with your intentions, creating personalized tools for rituals and ambiance.
- **Jewelry Making:** Create adornments featuring sacred symbols like the Ankh, infinity signs, or lotus flowers.
- **Nature Crafts:** Gather natural materials to make decor, such as flower crowns, pressed flower art, or handmade journals.

### 5. Nature-Inspired Creativity

- **Photography:** Capture the beauty of nature as a metaphor for your own growth and transformation.
- **Gardening:** Design a sacred garden space as a living expression of your creative energy and connection to nature.
- **Herbal Blending:** Develop teas, bath soaks, or essential oil blends inspired by your inner journey.

### 6. Spiritual Creativity

- **Sacred Symbol Design:** Draw or carve sacred symbols that resonate with your spiritual journey, such as a personalized sigil for self-love.
- **Affirmation Art:** Write affirmations in artistic scripts and frame them to remind you of your intentions.
- **Altar Art:** Design pieces specifically for your altar, such as paintings, sculptures, or small woven textiles.

# ENERGY TRANSMUTATION

Transforming sexual energy into creative energy that fuels art, purpose, and meaningful pursuits.

## Transmuting Celibacy into Creativity: Suggestions for Creative Pursuits

Choosing celibacy empowers you to focus your energies on creative pursuits. This practice allows you to truly connect with your inner essence and express it externally through painting, writing, music, and other forms of creativity. Here are some ideas for using your conserved energy to cultivate creativity and self-expression.

### 7. Culinary Arts

- **Sacred Cooking:** Use your energy to create meals with intentionality, blending ingredients that symbolize love, healing, and vitality.
- **Creative Presentation:** Experiment with plating or decorating your dishes to transform them into edible works of art.
- **Recipe Creation:** Develop unique recipes inspired by your emotions and energy flow.

### 8. Community and Shared Creativity

- **Workshops or Classes:** Share your creative journey by teaching others through workshops on journaling, art, or mindful movement.
- **Collaborative Projects:** Partner with like-minded individuals to co-create art, music, or rituals that honor self-love and celibacy.
- **Social Media Content:** Share your creations online to inspire and connect with a broader community.

## Affirmations for Creative Flow

As you engage in creative pursuits, affirm your connection to this divine energy:

- **My creative energy flows freely and abundantly.**

- **Through creativity, I honor my journey of self-love and celibacy.**

- **Each act of creation brings me closer to my authentic self.**

# ENERGY TRANSMUTATION

Transforming sexual energy into creative energy that fuels art, purpose, and meaningful pursuits.

## Integrating Creativity into Your Rituals

Incorporating creativity into your rituals strengthens your connection to your inner self and elevates the divine nature of your activities. Here are some ideas for incorporating creative energy into your daily or weekly rituals, making them unique to you.

1. **Morning or Evening Creative Ritual**

- **Start with Intention:** Light a candle or incense while setting an intention for your creative practice (e.g., "Today, I create with love and authenticity").
- **Journaling Ritual:** Begin your day or wind down at night by journaling your thoughts, dreams, or affirmations. Use colorful pens or draw symbols to amplify your intention.
- **Nature Sketching:** Spend time observing the sunrise or sunset and sketch or write about your impressions to connect with the rhythms of nature.

2. **Altar Creation as an Ongoing Art Project**

- **Dynamic Altar Design:** Treat your altar as a living artwork. Regularly change its layout with new crystals, symbols, or handmade items that reflect your current intentions or creative projects.
- **Seasonal Themes:** Incorporate elements like dried flowers, leaves, or candles in colors aligned with the season. Add handcrafted decor such as woven mats or painted stones.

3. **Creative Meditation Practices**

- **Mandala Meditation:** Create a mandala before or after meditation, using materials like sand, colored pencils, or natural objects. Each layer of your design can symbolize an aspect of your journey.
- **Affirmation Art Practice:** Meditate on affirmations while writing or painting them. Let the colors and brushstrokes flow intuitively, guided by your feelings.

4. **Sacred Movement as Creative Expression**
- **Ritual Dance:** Dedicate a specific time for movement that reflects your intentions. Let your body express joy, love, or release through freeform dance. Use scarves or ribbons to add an artistic element.
- **Yoga or Stretching:** Combine movement with creative visualization—imagine your energy as colors or shapes while transitioning between poses.

# ENERGY TRANSMUTATION

Transforming sexual energy into creative energy that fuels art, purpose, and meaningful pursuits.

## Integrating Creativity into Your Rituals

Incorporating creativity into your rituals strengthens your connection to your inner self and elevates the divine nature of your activities. Here are some ideas for incorporating creative energy into your daily or weekly rituals, making them unique to you.

5. **Ritual Bath with Artistic Elements**

- **Sacred Soaks:** Create an artistic ritual by arranging flowers, herbs, or essential oils in patterns around the tub. Use floating candles to illuminate your bathwater, symbolizing your creative spark.
- **Water Art:** Write affirmations or designs on waterproof paper or stones and place them in the water to infuse your bath with intention.

6. **Incorporating Music and Sound**

- **Custom Playlists:** Curate a playlist of music or natural sounds that inspire creativity and play it during rituals. For example, pair calming music with candle rituals or uplifting songs during dance.
- **Instrumental Exploration:** Use instruments like chimes, drums, or singing bowls to create soundscapes during meditation or as part of your ritual setup.

7. **Creative Offerings**

- **Handmade Offerings:** Craft items like small bundles of herbs, origami, or baked goods to offer during rituals of gratitude or release. These can symbolize your creative energy and intentions.
- **Symbolic Placement:** Place these offerings on your altar, in nature, or as a token to someone in need of encouragement.

8. **Vision Boarding as a Ritual**

- **Monthly Vision Ritual:** Dedicate time each month to create a vision board that aligns with your intentions. Use images, affirmations, and small sketches to represent your goals and inspirations.
- **Integration into Altar:** Display your vision board near your altar, updating it as you manifest and evolve.

# ENERGY TRANSMUTATION

Transforming sexual energy into creative energy that fuels art, purpose, and meaningful pursuits.

## Integrating Creativity into Your Rituals

Incorporating creativity into your rituals strengthens your connection to your inner self and elevates the divine nature of your activities. Here are some ideas for incorporating creative energy into your daily or weekly rituals, making them unique to you.

### 9. Nature Walks with Creative Energy

- **Gathering Materials:** Collect leaves, feathers, or stones to use in creative projects or rituals. Each item can hold the energy of your walk and intention.
- **Nature Journaling:** Sit in a serene spot and sketch or write about what you see and feel, letting your surroundings inspire you.

### 10. Celibacy as a Creative Ritual

- **Energy Transmutation Practice:** Sit quietly and visualize the energy of celibacy flowing upward, filling your heart and mind with creative inspiration. Allow this energy to guide your artistic or spiritual projects.
- **Creative Gratitude Ritual:** Write or paint a heartfelt expression of gratitude for the clarity and focus celibacy has brought into your life. Display this on your altar or keep it in a sacred space.

## Affirmations for Creative Ritual

- I create from a space of love and authenticity.

- My creative energy flows in harmony with my spiritual path.

- Every act of creation is a celebration of my divine essence

> Self-Love and Empowerment, two transformative energies that can illuminate your journey and elevate your spirit.

@ Empress Nefertiti-Mumbi

# SELF-LOVE AND EMPOWERMENT

Nurturing self-worth involves prioritizing healing and joy, so deepening your sense of wholeness.

## Expanding Self-Love

Self-love is the foundation of your well-being and the path to realizing your potential.

### 1. Self-Love as a Daily Practice

- **Morning Ritual:** Begin your day by placing your hand over your heart and saying, *"I am worthy, I am whole, I am love."* This sets a positive tone for your day.
- **Gratitude Journaling:** List three things you love about yourself every evening.
- **Mirror Work:** Spend five minutes looking into your eyes in the mirror, affirming your worth and beauty.

### 2. Cultivating Self-Compassion

- **Release Judgment:** Whenever you catch yourself in self-criticism, pause and reframe with kindness.
- **Gentle Reminders:** Wear a bracelet or carry a token that reminds you to treat yourself gently.
- **Forgiveness Ritual:** Write a letter to yourself forgiving any perceived mistakes, and burn it as a symbol of release.

### 3. Sacred Self-Care

- Create a spa-like experience at home. Use essential oils, nourishing masks, and a peaceful setting.
- Engage in nourishing movements such as yoga, stretching, or intuitive dance to honor your body.

## Empowerment in Your Journey

Empowerment is about reclaiming your energy and stepping into your authentic power with confidence and grace.

### 1. Defining Personal Boundaries

- **Sacred No:** Practice saying no to anything that drains your energy.
- **Energy Shielding:** Visualize a radiant light surrounding you, protecting your energy.
- **Boundary Affirmations:** *"I honor myself by saying no when it doesn't align with my highest good."*

# SELF-LOVE AND EMPOWERMENT

Nurturing self-worth involves prioritizing healing and joy, so deepening your sense of wholeness.

### 2. Embracing Your Voice

- **Speak Your Truth:** Write or verbally express your desires, values, and beliefs.
- **Creative Outlets:** Channel your inner power through art, writing, or music that reflects your journey.
- **Empowering Words**: Choose language that uplifts. Replace *"I can't" with "I am learning to" and "I should" with "I choose to."*

### 3. Taking Inspired Action

- Break larger goals into smaller, achievable steps to cultivate confidence.
- Celebrate every victory, no matter how small.
- Seek opportunities to uplift others—empowerment grows when shared.

## Bridging Self-Love and Empowerment

When self-love and empowerment are integrated, they create a powerful synergy:

- **Affirmation:** *"I love myself deeply, and I have the courage to stand in my truth."*

- **Visualization Exercise:** Imagine yourself as a radiant being of light, standing tall and confident. Envision love and power flowing through you like rivers of gold.

- **Empowerment Through Self-Celebration:** Reflect on your achievements, write love notes to yourself, or design a vision board that embodies your highest self.

THE SACREDNESS OF SELF-LOVE

# LETTERS TO MYSELF

## JOURNAL

**Celibacy as Sacred Self-Love: Transmuting Energy into Divine Creativity**

THE SACREDNESS OF SELF-LOVE   TODAY'S DATE: _____   S M T W T F S

# *Letters to Myself*

A LETTER TO MY YOUNGER SELF:

_____
_____
_____
_____
_____
_____
_____
_____
_____
_____
_____
_____
_____
_____
_____
_____
_____
_____
_____
_____
_____
_____
_____
_____
_____

# Letters to Myself

A LETTER TO MY YOUNGER SELF:

# Letters to Myself

A LETTER TO MY YOUNGER SELF:

THE SACREDNESS OF SELF-LOVE  TODAY'S DATE: _____  S M T W T F S

# Letters to Myself

A LETTER TO MY YOUNGER SELF:

THE SACREDNESS OF SELF-LOVE        TODAY'S DATE: _____        S M T W T F S

# *Letters to Myself*

A LETTER TO MY CURRENT SELF:

# Letters to Myself

A LETTER TO MY CURRENT SELF:

# Letters to Myself

A LETTER TO MY CURRENT SELF:

THE SACREDNESS OF SELF-LOVE   TODAY'S DATE: _____   S M T W T F S

# *Letters to Myself*

A LETTER TO MY CURRENT SELF:

THE SACREDNESS OF SELF-LOVE    TODAY'S DATE: _____    S M T W T F S

# *Letters to Myself*

A LETTER TO MY FUTURE SELF:

_____
_____
_____
_____
_____
_____
_____
_____
_____
_____
_____
_____
_____
_____
_____
_____
_____
_____
_____
_____
_____
_____
_____
_____
_____
_____

## Letters to Myself

A LETTER TO MY FUTURE SELF:

## Letters to Myself

A LETTER TO MY FUTURE SELF:

THE SACREDNESS OF SELF-LOVE  TODAY'S DATE: _____  S M T W T F S

## *Letters to Myself*

A LETTER TO MY FUTURE SELF:

_____
_____
_____
_____
_____
_____
_____
_____
_____
_____
_____
_____
_____
_____
_____
_____
_____
_____
_____
_____
_____
_____
_____
_____
_____
_____
_____

# Celibacy

## Declaration, Anniversary & Affirmations

# Declaration of Celibacy: A Gift of Pure Love to Myself

With unwavering conviction and boundless love,
I honor the sacred commitment to celibacy—
A gift I give to myself, unmatched in its purity and grace.
In this vow, I embrace the essence of who I am,
Nurturing the divine within me and cherishing my soul's journey.

**Celibacy is my declaration of self-respect, self-love, and self-sovereignty.**
Through this choice, I cultivate clarity, strength, and boundless creativity.
I honor my body as a sacred temple, my heart as a divine sanctuary,
And my spirit as an infinite wellspring of wisdom and light.

This path is not one of deprivation, but of **empowerment**.
It is a conscious celebration of the limitless love I hold within,
The love that flows freely and infinitely from me, for me.

Today, I affirm my truth:
I am whole. I am worthy. I am radiant.
I am the creator of my joy, the keeper of my peace,
And the guardian of my energy.

In every moment, I choose love over fear,
Healing over hurt, and sovereignty over surrender.

I declare: **Celibacy is the purest form of love to oneself**,
A precious gift I honor today and always.

With this vow, I open my heart to all that serves my highest good
And release all that no longer aligns with my divine purpose.

In gratitude and reverence,
I celebrate the beautiful journey of becoming
My truest, most radiant self.

**Celibacy as Sacred Self-Love: Transmuting Energy into Divine Creativity 2024**
**@Empress Nefertiti-Mumbi**

# CELIBACY
## DECLARATION

Today, I celebrate the sacred path I have chosen. On this day, I honor the commitment I have made to myself—to grow, to heal, and to love fully and authentically. I acknowledge the strength and courage it has taken to walk this journey, and I embrace the profound peace, energy, and joy it has brought into my life.

This day is a reminder of my divine essence and the power within me. I celebrate the freedom, clarity, and creative abundance that flows from this sacred choice.
With a heart full of gratitude, I renew my promise to nurture my soul, honor my body, and hold space for love in its purest form. I rejoice in my journey and look forward to the limitless possibilities that lie ahead.

Today is my day of empowerment, celebration, and joy. I honor myself. I am radiant. I am whole.

_____

**NAME**  **DATE**

Empress Nefertiti-Mumbi

**The Sacredness of Self-Love**  **Chapter 04**

# CELIBACY ANNIVERSARY

A Celibacy Declaration honors and celebrates the yearlong journey of self-love, spiritual growth, and empowerment.

## Celibacy Anniversary Declaration

This could be read aloud, written in a notebook, or spoken as part of a celebratory ritual using candles, flowers, or symbolic symbols. The certificate is supplied at the end of this section. You are welcome to print or order a customized one at the sites listed below:

- buymeacoffee.com/EmpressNefertiti
- http://empressnefertitimumbikin.com

Today, I celebrate the sacred path I have chosen. On this day, I honor the commitment I have made to myself—to grow, to heal, and to love fully and authentically. I acknowledge the strength and courage it has taken to walk this journey, and I embrace the profound peace, energy, and joy it has brought into my life.

This day is a reminder of my divine essence and the power within me. I celebrate the freedom, clarity, and creative abundance that flows from this sacred choice.

With a heart full of gratitude, I renew my promise to nurture my soul, honor my body, and hold space for love in its purest form. I rejoice in my journey and look forward to the limitless possibilities that lie ahead.

Today is my day of empowerment, celebration, and joy. I honor myself. I am radiant. I am whole.

## Rituals for Your Celibacy Anniversary

**1. Sacred Bathing Ritual**

- **Purpose:** Cleanse, renew, and recharge.

**How-To:**

- Create a sacred space with candles, soft music, and aromatic essential oils like lavender, rose, or frankincense.
- Add rose petals, Epsom salt, or Himalayan salt to the water.
- Meditate during the bath, reflecting on your growth. Recite affirmations like, *"I am a vessel of love and creativity. My choices are sacred."*

**The Sacredness of Self-Love**             **Chapter 04**

# CELIBACY ANNIVERSARY

A Celibacy Declaration honors and celebrates the yearlong journey of self-love, spiritual growth, and empowerment.

## Rituals for Your Celibacy Anniversary

2. **Plant a "Tree of Renewal"**
   - **Purpose:** Symbolize growth and the roots of your commitment.

   How-To:
   - Plant a tree, shrub, or flower on your anniversary date.
   - Whisper your declaration into the soil as a way of grounding your intentions for the year ahead.

3. **Candle Lighting Ceremony**
   - **Purpose:** Celebrate the light within.

   How-To:
   - Light candles in colors that represent your journey: white for purity, pink for love, gold for empowerment.
   - Sit quietly, focusing on the flame, and visualize your future path radiating with joy and clarity.

4. **Journal Time Capsule**

   - **Purpose:** Document your reflections and intentions for the next year.

   How-To:
   - Write a heartfelt letter to your future self, celebrating your accomplishments and sharing hopes for the year ahead.
   - Seal it and plan to open it on the next anniversary.

5. **Movement Ritual**
   - **Purpose:** Release energy and celebrate your body.

   How-To:
   - Practice a free-flowing dance, yoga, or any movement that connects you to your body.
   - Play empowering music that makes you feel alive and joyful.

The Sacredness of Self-Love                                    Chapter 04

# CELIBACY ANNIVERSARY

A Celibacy Declaration honors and celebrates the yearlong journey of self-love, spiritual growth, and empowerment.

## Gifts to Honor Yourself

**1. A Custom Piece of Jewelry**
- **Symbolize:** Your journey, like a ring or necklace with a meaningful charm (e.g., an ankh, heart, or infinity symbol).

**2. A Self-Care Day**
- **Plan:** Indulge in a spa day, massage, or something that makes you feel pampered and cherished.

**3. A Creative Gift**
- Paint or draw something that represents your growth. Or, treat yourself to art supplies, a musical instrument, or anything that supports your creativity.

**4. Sacred Object for Your Altar**
- **Examples:** A crystal, statue, or a meaningful object like a handmade candle or incense holder.

**5. A New Journal**
- Begin the next chapter of your journey with a fresh journal, perhaps engraved with words like "Sacred Journey" or "Empowerment Within."

**6. Personalized Book Collection**
- Gift yourself a book (or several!) that inspires your mind and spirit.

**7. A Solo Retreat**
- Plan a day or weekend getaway to reflect, meditate, and recharge in nature or a peaceful space.

## Celebration Feast

Prepare or treat yourself to a meal that will nourish both your body and soul.

Include things that hold spiritual and festive meaning for you, such as fresh fruits, herbal teas, or your favorite vegan a dish.

# CELIBACY ANNIVERSARY

A Celibacy Declaration honors and celebrates the yearlong journey of self-love, spiritual growth, and empowerment.

## Celibacy Anniversary, blending celebration, self-honor, and deeper connection:

### 1. Sacred Preparation
- **Cleanse Your Space:** Begin by tidying and energetically cleansing your space with incense or sage. Choose calming scents like frankincense, sandalwood, or lavender.
- **Set Up Your Altar:** Place your celibacy declaration certificate on your altar, surrounded by meaningful symbols like candles, crystals, flowers, and sacred objects that resonate with your journey.

### 2. Personal Rituals

**Morning Reflection**

- Light a white or gold candle to symbolize purity, transformation, and renewal.
- Sit quietly and meditate on the year's journey—what you've overcome, what you've discovered, and the love you've cultivated for yourself.

**Journaling Session**

*Reflect on the following prompts:*
- What have I learned about myself this past year?
- How has celibacy strengthened my spirit, body, and mind?
- What do I hope to nurture in the next year of this sacred journey?

*Write a love letter to your future self, celebrating who you are becoming.*

**Affirmation Ritual**

*Recite affirmations in front of a mirror, such as:*
- *"I honor the sacredness of my journey."*
- *"I am a vessel of love, creativity, and divine energy."*
- *"Each day, I grow more aligned with my highest self."*

# The Sacredness of Self-Love                    Chapter 04

# CELIBACY ANNIVERSARY

A Celibacy Declaration honors and celebrates the yearlong journey of self-love, spiritual growth, and empowerment.

## Celibacy Anniversary, blending celebration, self-honor, and deeper connection:

### 3. Creative Celebration
- **Art or Craft:** Create something meaningful—a painting, a piece of jewelry, or a vision board—that symbolizes your growth and aspirations.
- **Sacred Dance:** Put on music that uplifts your soul and move freely, expressing joy and gratitude.

### 4. Ritual Offerings
- **Plant a Seed:** Literally plant a flower, herb, or tree as a symbol of your continued growth. Nurture it throughout the year.
- **Crystal Programming:** Hold a crystal like rose quartz or amethyst and set intentions for your upcoming year of celibacy and self-love.

### 5. Gifts to Yourself
- **Self-Care Treats:** Invest in something luxurious, like an organic skincare set, a comfortable robe, or a beautiful journal.
- **Symbolic Jewelry:** Purchase or make a piece of jewelry (e.g., an ankh necklace) to wear as a daily reminder of your sacred commitment.

### 6. Evening Ritual
- **Sacred Bath:** End your day with a soothing bath infused with rose petals, lavender, and Himalayan salt. Add candles and soft music for a deeply meditative experience.
- **Gratitude Prayer:** Say a prayer or write a gratitude list, thanking the Divine, your ancestors, or the universe for guiding you and protecting your sacred path.

### 7. Closing with Intention

To conclude your ritual, gently extinguish the candle with a snuffer or by carefully covering it to cut off its oxygen supply. This practice symbolizes a peaceful closing, sealing your intentions with care and respect for the sacred space you've created.
- **Intention:** *"May this next year bring me deeper wisdom, unwavering peace, and abundant love."*
- Feel the glow of accomplishment, love, and hope as you complete your ritual.

# AFFIRMATIONS FOR SACRED COMMITMENT TO YOURSELF

Sacred Commitment to Yourself affirmation is infused with love and the harmony of both feminine and masculine energies:

**S — SACRED**
"My energy is sacred, and I channel it with intention and purpose to create a life filled with love, peace, and joy."

**A — ALL OF CREATION**
"By honoring myself, I honor the divine spark within all of creation."

**F — FULFILLMENT**
"I am the source of my own fulfillment, and my sacred energy blossoms in wholeness and light."

**E — EMBRACE**
"I embrace the divine balance of feminine and masculine energies within me, creating harmony and strength in my being."

**W — WORTHY**
"I am worthy of deep love and respect, and I give that to myself every single day."

**C — COMMITMENT**
"My commitment to myself is a reflection of my sacred essence, which I nurture with devotion and grace."

**H — HONOR**
"I honor my body, mind, and spirit as a sacred temple of infinite love and wisdom."

**S — SELF-LOVE**
"Through self-love, I align with the divine and open my heart to endless possibilities."

**Celibacy as Sacred Self-Love: Transmuting Energy into Divine Creativity**

# SAFEWCHS MANTRA FOR SACRED COMMITMENT TO YOURSELF

Sacred Commitment to Yourself affirmation is infused with love and the harmony of both feminine and masculine energies:

**S — SACRED**
Honoring the divinity within yourself.

**A — ALL OF CREATION**
Recognizing your connection to the universe.

**F — FULFILLMENT**
Embracing your journey with purpose and intention.

**E — EMBRACE**
Holding space for your growth and imperfections with love.

**W — WORTHY**
I honor my worth.

**C — COMMITMENT**
Staying dedicated to your self-love and healing journey.

**H — HONOR**
Respecting your worth and truth unapologetically.

**S — SELF-LOVE**
The foundation of your sacred connection to life.

SAFEWCHS (A POETIC REARRANGEMENT THAT IMPLIES "SAFE WISHES" OR "SAFETY WITHIN")

## Safewchs Mantra

I honor the Sacred within me,

In All Creation, I am free.

Fulfillment flows, my heart's embrace,

Commitment guides me in this space.

I Honor my worth, I rise above,

In Self-Love, I live, I love!

Safewchs Mantra is also on YouTube
@Empress Nefertiti-Mumbi Topic

**Celibacy as Sacred Self-Love: Transmuting Energy into Divine Creativity**

# AFFIRMATIONS FOR CREATIVITY

I am a channel for divine creativity, and inspiration flows through me effortlessly.

↑

CREATIVITY

Every idea I birth is infused with love, originality, and meaning. ←

→ My creative energy is abundant, limitless, and aligned with my highest purpose.

↙ My creativity blossoms when I honor the sacred rhythms of my mind, body, and spirit.

↘ I trust my intuition to guide me in expressing my unique gifts to the world.

# AFFIRMATIONS FOR EMPOWERMENT

> **I STAND FIRMLY IN MY POWER AND MAKE DECISIONS WITH CLARITY AND CONFIDENCE.**

> **I AM COURAGEOUS, RESILIENT, AND UNSTOPPABLE IN PURSUING MY DREAMS**

> **MY VOICE IS POWERFUL, AND MY PRESENCE MAKES A DIFFERENCE IN THE WORLD.**

> **I ATTRACT OPPORTUNITIES AND PEOPLE THAT UPLIFT AND EMPOWER ME.**

> **I TRUST IN MY DIVINE PURPOSE AND BOLDLY STEP INTO MY GREATNESS.**

**Celibacy as Sacred Self-Love: Transmuting Energy into Divine Creativity**

# AFFIRMATIONS FOR HEALING

I release all that no longer serves me and welcome peace into my being.

My heart is open to receiving the divine energy that heals me inside and out

I honor my healing journey with patience, compassion, and love.

Every breath I take renews and strengthens my body, mind, and spirit.

My body is a vessel of light and is continually healing and restoring itself.

# AFFIRMATIONS FOR SELF-LOVE

I DEEPLY AND UNCONDITIONALLY LOVE MYSELF, EXACTLY AS I AM.

I AM ENOUGH, AND I CELEBRATE MY UNIQUE BEAUTY AND ESSENCE.

EACH DAY, I NURTURE MY SOUL WITH LOVING THOUGHTS AND ACTIONS.

LOVING MYSELF IS THE GREATEST GIFT I GIVE TO THE WORLD.

I HONOR MY NEEDS AND TREAT MYSELF WITH CARE AND KINDNESS.

# AFFIRMATIONS FOR SELF-FORGIVENESS

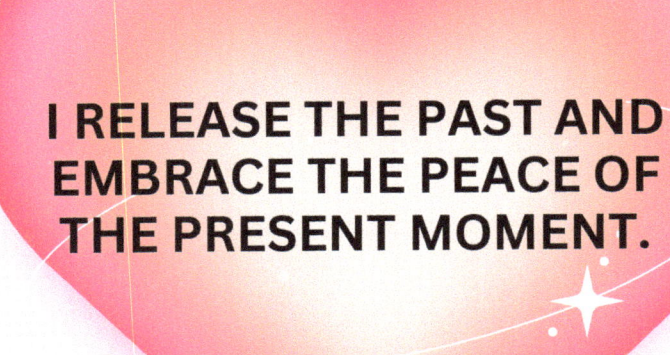

**I RELEASE THE PAST AND EMBRACE THE PEACE OF THE PRESENT MOMENT.**

I FORGIVE MYSELF FOR ALL THAT I DID NOT KNOW BEFORE; I GROW STRONGER EVERY DAY.

I AM WORTHY OF LOVE AND COMPASSION, ESPECIALLY MY OWN.

I LET GO OF GUILT AND SHAME AND REPLACE THEM WITH UNDERSTANDING AND KINDNESS.

I HONOR MY JOURNEY, INCLUDING THE MISTAKES THAT HAVE SHAPED MY GROWTH.

I ACCEPT MYSELF FULLY, WITH ALL MY IMPERFECTIONS AND STRENGTHS.

I TRUST MY ABILITY TO LEARN FROM THE PAST AND CREATE A BRIGHTER FUTURE.

I FORGIVE MYSELF FOR THE TIMES I DOUBTED MY WORTH; I AM ENOUGH JUST AS I AM.

I AM PATIENT WITH MYSELF AS I CONTINUE TO EVOLVE AND HEAL.

I CHOOSE TO HEAL BY RELEASING RESENTMENT TOWARD MYSELF AND OTHERS.

**Celibacy as Sacred Self-Love: Transmuting Energy into Divine Creativity**

# Affirmations for Protection

I am divinely protected, surrounded by light and love at all times.

My energy is sacred, and I create healthy boundaries to honor it.

I trust the universe to shield me from harm and negativity.

I walk through life with the strength of divine protection guiding me.

The love I carry within is my greatest shield and sanctuary.

I attract positive energy and repel anything that does not serve my highest good.

I invoke the protective power of the earth, sky, and cosmos to guide me each day.

With every breath, I ground myself in safety and peace..

I am a vessel of light; nothing can dim my inner glow.

I release all fears and embrace the protective grace of the universe.

*Celibacy as Sacred Self-Love: Transmuting Energy into Divine Creativity*

# AFFIRMATIONS FOR RATIONALITY

Rationality embodies clarity, discernment, and balanced decision-making. Guiding you toward grounding your thoughts and aligning them with your highest self.

These affirmations can serve as anchors, grounding your energy and helping you navigate life with a balanced perspective of intellect and intuition.

⭐ I trust my ability to think clearly and make decisions with wisdom and discernment.

🌿 I honor my mind as a sacred tool for understanding and navigating my journey.

☀️ I balance my emotions and thoughts to create harmony within and around me.

🌷 My choices reflect my inner truth, logic, and alignment with my highest good.

🌙 I let go of confusion and embrace the clarity that guides me toward my purpose.

⭐ My rational mind and intuitive heart work together in perfect harmony.

🌿 I approach challenges with calmness, reason, and confidence.

☀️ I am the master of my thoughts, choosing clarity and wisdom in every moment.

🌷 I trust the process of contemplation and seek understanding with patience.

🌙 I release overthinking and embrace simplicity, focus, and peace.

# Conclusion: A Sacred Beginning

As you close this chapter of The Sacredness of Self-Love, take a moment to honor the journey you've embarked on. Through reflection, self-discovery, and sacred rituals, you have begun to uncover the essence of your being—a wellspring of love, strength, and wisdom that resides within you. This is not just an ending but a profound beginning, an awakening to the infinite possibilities of your sacred self.

Each practice and affirmation you've embraced is a step toward deeper healing and empowerment. You've connected with the essence of celibacy as a gift to yourself, nurtured your inner light, and laid a foundation of self-love that will guide you through life's ever-changing landscapes. You've reclaimed your power, set intentions for your highest good, and begun to align with the universal truth of your worthiness.

Now, as you stand on this threshold, a new journey calls—a journey into healing and rediscovery. In Book Two: Healing and Rediscovery, you will be invited to explore the layers of your soul, releasing what no longer serves you and welcoming transformation. Together, we'll uncover tools and wisdom to heal past wounds, reconnect with your authentic self, and rediscover the joy of living in alignment with your true essence.

Let your heart remain open, your spirit curious, and your intentions sacred. The path ahead is one of empowerment, growth, and profound inner peace. You are ready for this next step, and the universe lovingly guides you forward.

With love and light,

Your Sacred Journey Awaits.

**Empress Nefertiti-Mumbi**

## Contact:

**Email:**
SacredEssencePress@proton.me

**Site:**
http://empressnefertitimumbikin.com

## SACRED ECHOES - A MUSICAL JOURNEY OF SELF-LOVE AND HEALING

*Sacred Echoes* is more than an album—it is a vibrational experience, an immersion into the depths of self-love, healing, and divine remembrance. Consisting of 13 soul-infused songs, each composition resonates at **432 Hz**, a frequency known for its harmonizing and restorative properties.

Born from the sacred journey of celibacy and self-discovery, every lyric and melody was divinely inspired to uplift, empower, and guide both myself and others through the transformative path of self-love, renewal, and spiritual awakening. Just as *Pure Essence: Embracing Celibacy as a Path to Self-Love and Healing* offers wisdom through words, Sacred Echoes offers healing through sound, acting as a sacred companion to the book series.

Each song is infused with intention, channeling love and divine frequencies to awaken the soul, soothe the heart, and deepen the connection with one's true essence. Whether through meditation, reflection, or simple moments of stillness, this album is an invitation to align with the sacredness within.

**Listen to Sacred Echoes** on YouTube:
*Empress Nefertiti-Mumbi - Topic*
**All** Main Music Outlets: *Apple, Spotify,Tidal and ect..*

May this music serve as a guiding light on your journey to self-love, healing, and the infinite embrace of your divine essence.

# NOTES

**1. Honoring Your Inner Self as Sacred**

"Your inner self is a sacred sanctuary, deserving of love, attention, and reverence. By viewing yourself as sacred, you open the door to deeper healing and transformation."

Citation: Megre, V. (1996–2006). The Ringing Cedars of Russia series. Ringing Cedars Press.

**2. Developing a Deeper Relationship with Yourself**

"When you cultivate a deeper connection with yourself, you unlock the layers of your inner being, learning to listen, heal, and grow."

Citation: Brown, B. (2010). The Gifts of Imperfection. Hazelden Publishing.

**3. Creating Rituals for Self-Connection**

"Rituals like lighting candles, journaling, or meditating create a sacred space where you can nurture your relationship with yourself."

Citation: Chopra, D. (2000). The Seven Spiritual Laws of Success. Amber-Allen Publishing.

**4. The Essence of Celibacy**

"Celibacy is not just abstaining from sexual relations but is a profound journey of channeling energy into self-discovery and creativity."

Citation: Kelly, E. (2020). The Art of Celibacy: Spiritual Power Through Self-Mastery. Self-published.

# Pure Essence: Embracing Celibacy as a Path to Self-Love and Healing

The Pure Essence series invites readers on a transformative journey through the sacred realms of self-love, healing, and spiritual growth. Across its five books—The Sacredness of Self-Love, Healing and Rediscovery, Living in Harmony with Nature, The Power of Feminine Energy, and The Power of Masculine Energy—this series gently guides individuals to reconnect with their authentic selves through the profound practice of celibacy.

Each volume is a stepping stone, offering tools, reflections, and rituals that honor the wholeness of the human spirit. The books aim to inspire a new understanding of celibacy— not as deprivation, but as a sacred commitment to one's growth, creativity, and inner harmony. Together, they nurture a balance of feminine and masculine energies, fostering a deep-rooted connection to one's essence and the universe.

In The Sacredness of Self-Love, readers explore the foundation of self-respect and personal boundaries, discovering how celibacy becomes a declaration of love for oneself. Moving into Healing and Rediscovery, they delve into releasing past wounds and stepping into a space of renewal.

Living in Harmony with Nature reconnects readers to the rhythms of the earth, embracing its nurturing energies to amplify their spiritual path. The Power of Feminine Energy illuminates the creative, intuitive, and nurturing aspects of the self, while The Power of Masculine Energy celebrates strength, action, and purpose with equal reverence.

By the conclusion of this journey, the Pure Essence series becomes more than a guide—it transforms into a companion for life. Readers are empowered to embrace celibacy as a holistic practice, blending spirituality, self-awareness, and healing into every facet of their existence. It encourages celebration, reflection, and self-honoring at every milestone, reminding us all that true love begins within.

With each turn of the page and each journal entry completed, the reader takes a step closer to the purest version of themselves, living as a radiant expression of love, peace, and balance in the world.

Let this series be a light on your path, a reminder that your essence is sacred, your journey is unique, and your capacity for growth and love is infinite.